TRAINING YOUR YOUNG CHOIR

by

David Bramhall

*To Ipswich Girls' Choir, the Suffolk Jubilee Choir
and The Harmony Girls' Choir, who taught me all I know.*

*With grateful thanks to my very experienced friends and
colleagues Christine Laughlin, Carol Sturdy and Mary Bishop-Hunt
for their helpful suggestions on early-years singing.*

Training your young choir, Second Edition 2010
Copyright © 2010 David Bramhall
First published in 2001 by The Choirmaster Press

*The moral right of David Bramhall to be identified as the author of this work has
been asserted in accordance with the Copyright, Designs and Patents Act 1988*

*The extract from John Gardner's Waly Waly is © Oxford University Press 1971
and is reproduced with their kind permission*

CONTENTS

The last few years have seen an upsurge of interest in young people singing, whether in school or in extra-curricular choirs. Partly this has been due to the popularity and media coverage of such events as, in the UK, the Sainsbury's (now The BBC) "Choir of the Year" Competition, which revealed youth choirs of quite breathtaking quality. New initiatives by one or two music publishers have provided fresh and entertaining material that young people can enjoy, and the music industry in general has seen an increase in the different genres of music available on CD. Importantly, in the UK the National Curriculum for Music now requires that singing be a part of the educational diet of all children up to age 14. More and more teachers, especially in first (primary) schools, are having to involve themselves in singing, and this book aims to help them as well as those lucky enough to be working with more advanced choirs.

There is much in this book that will annoy some people. My suggestions about rehearsal technique will irritate many choir-trainers who do things differently themselves. My thoughts on articulation and expression will arouse derision among the purists. My ideas of vocal technique will probably make singing teachers see red. All I can say is that I've been training young people's choirs for a very long time, that I love it and think about it constantly, that I never tire of trying new ideas, that my choirs sing well and to their own great satisfaction, that I have never damaged a young person's voice so far as I know, and that these are the things that work for me. You'll just have to make up your own mind!

PRELUDE - SINGING IN THE PRIMARY SCHOOL

I had thought to start by talking of the people - we have all met them - who were put off singing at an early age because they were told "You can't sing" or "You can't sing in tune" or even "You're spoiling it, so just sit at the back and keep quiet!", but that's such a hairy old cliché it would be an insult to the reader's intelligence.

So let's cut to the chase ....

... every child CAN sing and every child SHOULD sing.

What little children can and can't do

Most children can naturally sing within the range Middle C up to G or A, and often seem particularly attached to "me" and "soh" (E and G in the key of C, or F sharp and A in the key of D).

However, you will find some who can sing quite well below that, but can't manage within that range. Or there are some who can sing quite well high up, but not down below. These will be what are sometimes called "groaners", although the truth is that they simply haven't yet learned to control a particular part of their voices. It is possible that, if we were to pitch our songs in the appropriate range for them, they could sing perfectly well in tune - unfortunately, that would leave the rest floundering!

So the only recourse is to use games and exercises to help all children find their way round their voices - and NEVER make an issue of singing in or out of tune. It is not important. The more they sing and the more they enjoy it, the better they will get. In nearly all cases, in time, the problem will just go away by itself. There are some children who can sing a whole phrase but can't copy a single note, but as virtually all songs require them to sing phrases and not single notes this hardly seems important, does it?

People often speak of children being "tone deaf", but in fact there is no such thing as "tone deafness" - or if there is, it must be very rare indeed. If you were really tone deaf you wouldn't recognise a police siren, and you wouldn't be able to distinguish one pop song from another – and all children can do that. If you were really tone deaf you would be unable to tell whether a note had gone up or down in pitch, and virtually every child can do that too. They may not know the correct name to use - they might not be able to relate the word "up" to a note of higher pitch or the word "down" to a lower one (it's quite common for them to say it's got louder or softer instead) - but they can tell you when the note has changed, which means they are not "tone deaf".

The main thing that causes children to arrive in school "unable" to sing, is that they come from homes where nobody sings. Perhaps they don't listen to music either, as the two usually go hand in hand. The answer is very simple - supply that need in school by singing a lot, all the time, as a matter of routine. In this chapter we will look at some ways of making singing a normal thing to do in school.

The early years - what should we try to achieve?
To make singing normal in your school you, the teacher, must sing yourself. You don't have to be a good singer. You don't have to be trained. You don't necessarily have to be able to read music very well. You don't have to be able to sing a lot of high notes. Even if you think you can't sing in tune, you can probably manage as long as you avoid singing against an instrument - young children won't notice. So long as you can keep pace with the children and select material that suits you from the wealth of publications available, you'll be all right - you just need the nerve to do it!

Do bear in mind that you will teach the best, what you know best. Songs you remember from your own childhood will still be perfectly appropriate, and because you know them so well you will teach them with ease and fluency.

There is a school of thought in the musical world that turns its nose up at "old", well-loved music and searches for material at the margins instead. I think this is a mistake, although certainly one should not be afraid to try new things. Despite the fact that many experienced adult orchestral musicians are thoroughly bored by Beethoven's 5th Symphony, it is nevertheless a great piece of music that has stood the test of time, and every young orchestral player ought to perform it at least once. I have always thought that the old chestnut *Nymphs and Shepherds* was a jolly good tune that ought still to be performed by children as it often was in the 1930s and 1940s. Sadly and to my shame, I have never quite summoned up the nerve to do it. I *have* used Thomas Arne's *Where the bee sucks, there suck I* in class with twelve-year-olds, and it was very popular. At the very least, using songs you know well yourself will help you get started and give you time to search for new material.

Some of the most effective methods of making singing a matter of routine involve things like the alphabet, multiplication tables and the class register, so it's best if other teachers in the school are willing to take the plunge too. If you can't play the piano yourself, perhaps there's a mother who can? If she can only manage to learn a couple of songs, that's all right too. Your class can always do most of their singing without accompaniment and invite her in occasionally for a "special treat". Perhaps you could make a recording of her, to use when she can't be present? In fact, an instrument can often get in the way, for children pick up a melody most easily from another voice.

2

Young children have an enormous capacity for learning by rote and remembering what they have learnt. It's what their developing brains respond to best. As Sally Goddard Blythe wrote in the Times Educational Supplement (9/1/98) *"... the developing brain is particularly receptive to .... rote learning between the ages of 4 and 7½. It involves the developing right hemisphere of the cortex ... that learns to read by the whole word, look/say method"*.

Our aim should be to build up quite a large repertoire of useful songs - by which I mean songs that are carefully chosen to encourage the children to explore and become familiar with their voices, and which they will enjoy singing – and don't be too quick to judge children's enjoyment by their facial expressions: I have often been told by parents that their child who seems not to be participating in class, proudly performs whole songs to them at home.

Select songs with repetitive music and words. These will be easier to learn and remember, and children will find them more entertaining. They will also gain that all-important familiarity with their voices from which will come vocal control. Avoid songs which contain too many notes, large leaps, particularly high or low passages (unless these serve to illustrate part of a "story"), or that are musically complex. Here, for instance, is a song that is almost perfect for our purposes:

Subsequent verses go "Did you ever see a laddie" ... "a postman" .... "a policeman" .... "a teacher" etc. each with the appropriate actions.

This is a song that is repetitive and therefore easy to learn, offers the opportunity for simple yet entertaining actions, and by its constant repetition of "me-doh-doh" and "ray-soh-soh" makes singers practise first a small interval and then a larger one, moving from the middle to the bottom of the voice. There is a strong feeling of "doh" halfway through and at the end - an unconscious feeling for tonality is something else we wish to foster. There is opportunity for improvisation, for children love the game of changing one or two words for ideas of their own. The only drawback is that it has a range of a ninth which might be a bit much for the very youngest. This is just one example - the books suggested in the section on repertoire will contain dozens more.

Later in this book there is a detailed section on "teaching a song". For now, follow your natural instinct and do it by example. They will learn faster if you sing to them, not play on the piano. Sing each phrase in turn, then let them sing it with you. Pick out interesting things about the tune – repeated words or musical phrases, places where there are a lot of notes on one word, big leaps, onomatopoeia (where the music mirrors or imitates the meaning in some way) etc. - and practise them separately. Don't let them become bored: you don't have to learn the whole song in one sitting - save some for next week! If your singing session lasts, say, thirty minutes, don't spend more than ten minutes learning new material if you can help it.

If you teach songs to your classes without any accompaniment you must be careful about "pitching". Most teachers tend to sing songs at too low a pitch for the children because they find it easier themselves. Practise at home by yourself first. Sing the song at different pitches, first low, then high, then somewhere in between. What you are trying to achieve is a pitch that places the tune near the top of your own range so that you can just sing it comfortably (this may not be true if you are a counter-tenor or a *coloratura* soprano, but in that case you probably don't need my advice anyway).

The final thing to say in this section is that what we are NOT trying to achieve is strong, beautiful, accurate singing. This would be a wonderful achievement, but it is not practical in the early stages. What you seek to create is an environment where every child sings habitually and happily. If some are not very well in tune, so be it. If it isn't very loud, so be it - in fact, one often needs to restrain little children from overdoing it, for some enjoy themselves so much they become raucous. On the other hand, from an early stage they should be encouraged to listen to each other and to balance their singing with that of the others, so that everyone is making approximately the same amount of sound.

The importance of routine

Although you will obviously seek to introduce some dedicated singing sessions into your school week, it is important to establish the idea that singing is an every-day, routine activity. Your pupils should come to believe that everyone sings as a matter of course. The best way to do this is to link singing with the routine of school life, and the most obvious opportunity is in calling the register. The first time you do it will be something of a novelty, although if you have a new class at the beginning of the year they will simply accept it as one more new thing to do and be quite unsurprised. This activity should really be introduced when the pupils are very young, before they begin to develop that keen sense of embarrassment in the face of their peers.

Sing each child's name to a four note pattern like this .....

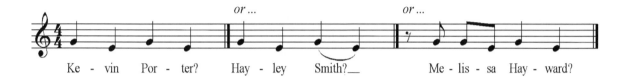

Each child answers like this ....

If a child is absent, the whole class will enjoy telling you ......

Just as one promotes individual reading in school, so individual singing should not be a major issue in your mind or those of the pupils. Naturally one will act quickly to discourage any hint of ridicule, but in my experience if the teacher behaves as though the activity is entirely normal, the children will think it is.

The notes illustrated (soh and me) seem to be the most natural for most children, but you will quickly sense that while some can just about cope, others find it too easy. For them, one could pose a more complex pattern to imitate. Here are a few examples .....

In order to reply to you, they will have to adapt notes and words slightly, and might need a little prompting at first. They'll soon get the hang of it, and already you've painlessly introduced the idea of improvisation.

Other common routines lend themselves to singing just as well. In the section below you will find suggestions for singing the alphabet and times tables, for instance. Or is yours one of the schools where children greet their teacher formally at the beginning of the day - "Good morning, Miss Westley" ..... "Good morning, class"? Why not sing it? Or do you have a little home-time ritual that would suit? Perhaps you might introduce one?

Always do things the same way each time, so that their responses and their attitudes to singing become a habit. Children love routine. I know one teacher who uses a tambourine to give signals in class - a shake and a tap for "Quiet now, and pay attention!", a descending shake for "Sit down!" and so on. I have heard another do the same thing with a swannee whistle which sounded silly but worked well enough.

I have also seen a teacher giving out percussion instruments with a charming ritual, chanting "I look in the box, now what have I got ....?" as she moved round the room.

In all your singing activities, whether routine ones or dedicated "singing lessons", you must expect different levels of response from different individuals at different times. Some children are enthusiastic about everything all the time, some are always negative, and most have "off days". Move quickly from one activity to another, vary them as much as possible (including movement: one activity can be performed seated, the next standing, the next walking round in a circle etc.), and beware seeking too much perfection. Do not try to ensure that every child completely understands or can fully achieve each activity. This is counter-productive: it will bore the children, it may frustrate you, and it will introduce the concept of failure in a context where there should be no such thing. Children who believe they are failing (to sing the right notes, to remember the words, to sing in tune, to sing high enough or whatever) will soon switch off. Move quickly, repeat often and competence will follow soon enough.

Sometimes you'll have to do most of the singing for them, perhaps because they haven't picked up the tune yet, or because they're busy with the movements that go with it. Encourage them to sing with you, of course, but avoid making a big deal of "Right, now you sing it without me!" and putting them on the spot. Better to wait until they seem fairly confident and just quietly drop out without drawing attention to it.

Similarly, avoid making an issue of "joining in" at all. It is quite common for a child to be having a sulk, or simply to decide that it wants to be different. Don't insist, but encourage some other sort of participation - by applauding, or by clapping in time, or perhaps just by listening.

When directing children to listen, always give them something to listen <u>for</u>, such as "Can I hear the words?" or "How many times can I hear a particular word?" or "Which is louder, the singing or the piano?" etc.

Do play recordings of vocal music to your pupils. Schools often use a wide variety of orchestral and other music (when going in to assembly, for instance) but ignore choral music. Children should become aware of the many different ways of using the voice - the western choral tradition, grand opera, blues, jazz and "scat", groups like the Trio Bulgarka and the various sounds of choirs from Africa, Russia, the South Seas etc. Not only will this provide possible role models, but it will encourage the idea of singing as a normal and everyday activity. Older children could also learn songs that were created for the specific purpose of accompanying routine work activities - negro spirituals, sea shanties and so on.

You may find that children find some styles amusing or silly, and they may poke fun at grand opera, say, or scat. I don't think this matters at all, and you shouldn't let it put you off. If they're making fun of it, at least they've listened to it and are aware of it, which was your intention. Besides, let's face it, there really <u>is</u> something slightly ridiculous about grand opera!

Do also try to establish a routine about posture. Too often one sees schoolchildren sitting cross-legged on the floor to sing, which cannot be a good thing if only because it will encourage lazy habits later on. They can sit down while they learn or talk about a song, or while listening to a recording, but should expect to stand up whenever they are going to do some serious singing.

Above all, in the early years one should embrace what may seem, to us adults, an endless and mindless repetition. Little children (and big ones, to some extent) enjoy routine because it makes them feel secure. They respond well to habitual responses because they don't need to think about them. We must use this natural propensity to help them assimilate the complex language of music without effort or explanation, safe in the knowledge that its components can be teased out and intellectualised at a later stage when they are ready.

The Mrs.Butcher Story, or A sneaky bit of voice-training ....

Young children usually (though not always) sing entirely in their chest or speaking voices, and a major problem is to enable them to go higher without "reaching up" and straining - in other words, they need to discover their "head voice". This can be taught quite easily provided you do NOT, ever, approach it from BELOW. Singing up and up a scale is the <u>worst</u> thing you can do.

I usually tell this little story about my own childhood ....

> *"I used to live in London, in a street of little terraced houses all joined together. The lady who lived next door was called Mrs.Butcher, a big fat lady who always wore a hairnet and had a very short husband called ..... well, of course, Mister Butcher! When Mrs.Butcher wanted to speak to my mother about something (usually to complain because I'd kicked my football over the fence and broken some of Mr.Butcher's tomato plants), she'd waddle down the garden a little way, lean over the fence so she could see our back door, and call "Oo-oo!" Can you do that?"*

> *"If my mother couldn't hear, Mrs.Butcher would call a bit louder: "Oo-oo! Oo-oo!" And eventually, as Mrs. Butcher had a very piercing voice, my mother couldn't pretend she hadn't heard and would have to come out and lean over the fence for what they called 'a bit of a chin-wag'."*

Now make the children imitate Mrs.Butcher and go "Oo-oo! Oo-oo!" Almost all of them will do it in their head voices quite naturally. What fun! Make sure they really are doing an "ooh" sound with a little round mouth. Then try it a little higher - "Come on, my mother still can't hear!" Gradually turn it into a little tune like this .....

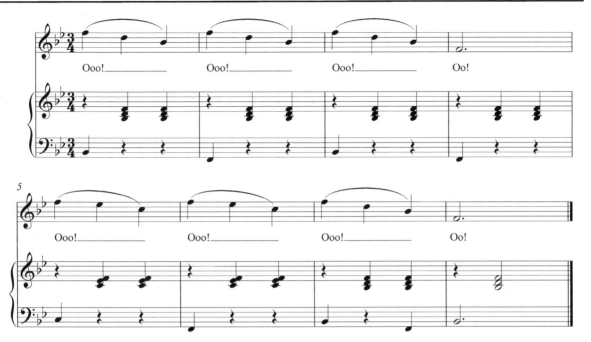

Notice that already, having got into the head voice, we are bringing it downwards to meet the chest voice. Try introducing a different vowel sound, or actually singing it to some nonsense words. If you keep taking it further and further down, some children may be able to tell you when they feel the change from one voice to the other. And afterwards, whenever you come across a high passage you'll only have to say "Mrs.Butcher!" and they'll remember how to do it.

A few early-years activities to get you started

In no particular order, here are a few suggested activities for very young pupils. None of them are original, and no doubt you will either think of better ones yourself, or find some in the publications I have suggested in the section on "repertoire".

- A useful way of warming up, having fun and banishing inhibitions is a "follow-my-leader" type of game involving non-singing mouth sounds - growling, rolling your rrr's, tongue-wagging-bubble-sounds, raspberries, glissandi etc. You have to be a bit of an actor yourself, and be sure that you can control the inevitable excitement! You don't have to be the leader all the time, of course - one of the children might like to do it.

- After each successful song or game, encourage them to give themselves a clap. Also encourage applause whenever an individual or a group does something on their own.

- Teacher (whispering, **pp**): *"Have you got a whispering voice?"*
  Pupils (also **pp**): *"This is my whispering voice!"*
  Teacher (speaking, **mp**): *"Have you got a speaking voice?"*
  Pupils (also **mp**): *"This is my speaking voice!"*
  Teacher (**mf**, singing on two notes): *"Have you got a singing voice?"*
  Pupils (also **mf**, on two notes): *"This is my singing voice!"*
  Teacher (very loudly, **ff**): *"Have you got a shouting voice?"*
  Pupils (also **ff**): *"This is my shouting voice!"* and so on, at your
  discretion - soft, loud, quick, slow, low, high etc.

Have you got a whisp' ring voice? This is my whisp' ring voice!

- Teacher (on two notes as before, at a
  medium pitch): *"Coo - ee, copy me"*
  Pupils (copying): *"Coo - ee, copy me"*
  Teacher (on two notes, at a low pitch): *"Coo - ee, copy me"*
  Pupils (copying): *"Coo - ee, copy me"*
  Teacher (on two notes, at a higher pitch): *"Coo - ee, copy me"*
  ..... and so on, perhaps varying the tone of voice (soft, gruff,
  spiky etc.) as well as the pitch, and later adding more notes.

- Have the children sit in a circle. Build a hum* round the circle,
  each child joining in as you indicate by moving round the circle.
  Raise your arms to invite a louder hum, and lower them to get
  softer. Make an abrupt sign to indicate that they should stop, and
  then by gesture make them start again. Do it all by gesture, without
  verbal instructions. Have them copy your gestures at the same time.
  Then ask one of them to stand in the middle and become the
  conductor - they'll think that's great fun.

  ** Humming is tiring on the voice. Much better to
  go "nnggg" with open mouths.*

- Let them march round the room in time with your beat on a
  tambourine or drum. Gradually change the speed. Or try hitting the
  tambourine hard so they have to stamp in time, and then playing
  very softly so that they tiptoe. Stop abruptly so they have to freeze
  until you start again. When they've had enough, a quick rattle on
  the tambourine can be the sign to run back to their seats. Not
  strictly a singing activity, of course, but a good way of instilling the
  essential feeling for pulse.

- Don't turn your nose up at the idea of using tunes like *Do the Hokey Cokey* which provide an opportunity for movement. They don't know how corny this is! At first you may have to do all the singing for them as they'll be busy thinking about the movements, but with repetition they'll begin to join in. A&C Black's *Okki-tokki-unga* is a treasure-house of suitable songs like *The grand old Duke of York, One finger one thumb, Nicky nacky knocky noo, This old man, The wheels on the bus, Heads shoulders knees and toes* and many more, with suggestions for movement games.

- A non-singing "pitch" game .....

    Three little monkeys swinging from a tree,
    Along came a crocodile (sshh!) *as quietly as can be.*
    (In a high monkey voice) *"Hey, Mr.Crocodile, you can't catch me!"*
    (In a deep crocodile voice) *"Grumph!"*

  Two little monkeys halfway up the tree,
  Along came a crocodile (sshh!) *as quietly as can be.*
  (In a high monkey voice) *"Hey, Mr.Crocodile, you can't catch me!"*
  (In a deep crocodile voice) *"Grumph!"*

    One little monkey at the top of the tree,
    Along came a crocodile (sshh!) *as quietly as can be.*
    (In a high monkey voice) *"Hey, Mr.Crocodile, you can't catch me!"*
    (In a deep crocodile voice) *"Grumph!"*
    (A bit higher) *"Grumph!"*
    (Even higher) *"Grumph!"*
    (Very high indeed) *"Grumph!"*
    (In a high monkey voice, mocking) *"Na, na-na nah nah!"*

- Look for any rhymes or songs to teach your pupils that mention "top" and "bottom", "up" and "down", or any other concepts that can be illustrated with the voice ("slide", "pop", "loud", "soft" etc.), or with movement ("this way" and "that way" etc.)

- Traditional skipping games and playground chants can be useful in the classroom.

- Children really enjoy improvisation and from an early age will readily add their own ideas to songs like *"She'll be coming (hopping, skipping, jumping etc.) round the mountain"* or extra instruments for *"I am the Music Man"*.

11

● If your pupils know, or are learning, the alphabet, let them sing it to a descending scale like this:

(this works well as a round, second group starting when the first group gets to "h")

● In many schools it is still normal practice to "chant" the times tables. If yours is one of them, combine it with singing. An obvious musical phrase to use is this ....

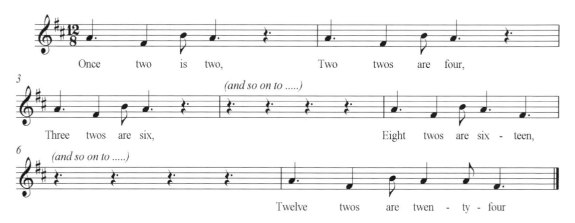

Other things to chant or sing are the days of the week and the months of the year.

● You can begin part-singing very early if one of the parts is a simple, repeated ostinato. For instance, many songs can stand being accompanied by a small group of children singing "soh, me, soh, me" over and over, or there might be some words that could be rhythmically chanted in the background.

Solfa and signing

One of the most influential musicians in 20th Century education was Zoltan Kodály, the Hungarian composer and academician. The British Kodály Academy (c/o 10 Lapwing Close, South Croydon, Surrey CR2 8TD, UK; tel.0044 208651 3728; website www.britishkodalyacademy.org) is a source of publications and courses on musical education through singing, including Early Childhood and Special Educational Need provision.

Central to the "Kodály method" is the art of "signing", using hand-signals to indicate each step of the solfa scale as follows ......

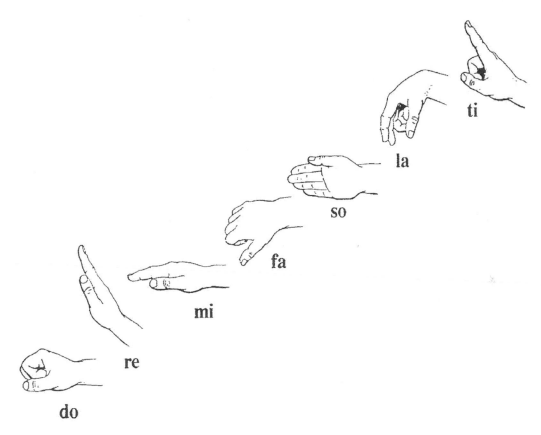

These signs originated not with Kodaly but in the famous Curwen Method, a refinement of the French art of *solfège.* They are an excellent and effective tool, especially if you encourage the children to sign back at you, thus developing a physical response to an aural concept. The use of solfa and signs combined can be of great benefit in building a repertoire of familiar intervals. Without it, a child may know that a particular song begins with a low note and then a higher one, but has no means of judging just how <u>much</u> higher. With sign/solfa, he or she can relate the song to an already familiar interval and will therefore sing it more readily and with far more accuracy.

However, a major problem for me is that some of the individual signs are inappropriate. Elsewhere in this book I will suggest that a downward palm is a "negative" sign that children instinctively interpret to mean "be quiet", and one that promotes flatness. On "me", the major third of a scale (the one note of the scale that needs to be bright and sharp if singing is to be in tune) the very last thing one should do is make a negative sign, although the downward palm does have a place to indicate the minor third, "mor", when it occurs. I therefore use an upturned palm for both "me" and "te". For the same reason I use a "thumbs up" sign for "la" and "fa". The duplication of signs is not a problem in practice: the children distinguish between them partly from the context, and partly because you make "fa" lower down, and "la" and "te" higher in the air. Well, you would, wouldn't you?

These signs can be introduced as a "game", using short melodic phrases to be sung and signed repetitively in imitation of the teacher. I came to "signing" relatively late in my teaching career, have found it amazingly easy and effective, and wish I'd learned it many years ago!

Using notation

The main purpose of musical notation is to act as an *aide memoire* to help you remember music you already know. It is only when we reach a fairly advanced stage that the element of "sight reading", i.e. singing or playing something we have never seen or heard before, becomes relevant. Therefore the most appropriate way of introducing young children to written music is to ask them to "guess" which familiar phrase you are showing them (of course it's not guessing really, but a rational interpretation of given information. But they don't need to know that). For instance, if your class already know the sign/solfa phrases given above, one could make a fine game of writing one of them on the white-board in staff notation instead, and asking them to "imagine" which one it is before singing it.

Later one could make up entirely new phrases using the same group of notes and ask them to imagine those before singing. This will be real sight-reading.

Many teachers would not attempt any sort of notation work with young children. Personally, I do: but I don't teach the <u>names</u> of the notes (D, E, F sharp etc.) at all, not for a very long time. It's far more important for them to become familiar with the notion that "up" on the stave means "up" in the voice. More factual information than that isn't helpful.

Neither do I attempt to teach note-values or note-names such as "crotchet = 1", "dotted crotchet = 1½", "minim = 2" and so on. Again, in these early stages this is unnecessary factual information (and it isn't even true - if you think about it, in 6/8 time a dotted crotchet is worth 1, not 1½). All they need to know is that white notes last longer than black ones. Indeed, I have teenagers in my choirs who can sight-read quite complex music very successfully but are not at all fluent in the "theory". As they are therefore able to use the written music for its intended purpose with considerable accuracy, I suggest that the "theory" is (for them, and at that stage) superfluous.

One should mainly work from the known to the unknown. In other words, for a long time I would not attempt to make them "read" music in the accepted sense, but simply use the staff notation to represent <u>what they have already learnt</u>. Once they have got the hang of recognising simple phrases, why not give them the beginning of an actual song they know, and ask them to decide which one it is before singing it? They will need a lot of help at first. It might go something like this ....

Miss Polly had a dolly

"Now, children, this is a tune we all know, and these are the notes written on the stave - that's these five lines here. They help us to tell how high or low a note is. Do you think the first note ..." (pointing) *"... is high or low or middling?"*

"Yes, it's a low note. What about the next? It's a bit higher, isn't it?"

"Now, look at this bit ..." (points to first bar. They don't know it's called a "bar" of course). *"There are lots of notes in this bit, aren't there, so they'll have to go quite quickly or they won't fit in. Can we think of a tune we know that starts on a low note, then has a lot of quick notes a bit higher up?"*

And so on. Once they have guessed the tune with your help, ask them to identify the notes that go with "sick, sick, sick" and "quick, quick, quick" or any other easily identifiable features. They could then tell you which note needed which word written underneath. A word of warning - they'll have difficulty with the idea that where a word has two syllables it will need two notes, because they probably haven't been introduced to the idea of a "syllable" yet. Still harder is the concept of a "melisma", or one word which spreads over several notes indicated by a slur sign, for example .....

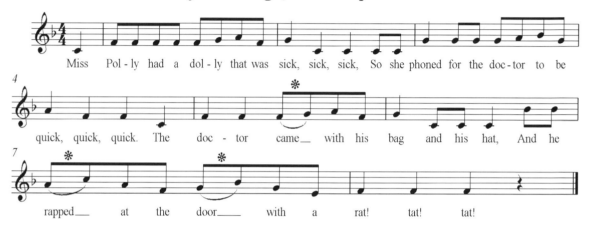

Of course, once you introduce written words with the written music, that makes a heavy demand on your pupils' reading skills, so think about it before you try – if they can't read the words easily, how do you expect them to do the music as well?.

Another approach is to use "graphic" or "pictorial" notation. This involves the use of shapes or lines on the black- or white-board, and offers a splendid opportunity for your pupils to invent their own symbols. They will soon realise that they can show "soft" with a small symbol, for instance, and "loud" with a big one. They will need to invent some means of indicating long or short duration, probably by using a short or long line which gets them used to the linear, left-to-right nature of the conventional notation they will be using later on. There are some ideas for graphic score work in my own book *"Composing in the Classroom Opus 1"* (Boosey & Hawkes 1989).

If you want to gently lead your classes into more conventional "sight-reading", try starting with this little song (you are welcome to make as many photocopies as you need). You have to divide the class into two halves, one on each line. Discuss it with them first – which are the longer notes? Where do they have to go up, and where down? How many times do the seconds have to sing "I don't"? and so on ...

A Smelly Song

The Thinking Voice

The "thinking voice" is something your pupils should begin to use quite early on. In other words, you should lead them to "imagine" the music without actually making a sound. Again, begin with material they already know. For instance, while singing *"Miss Polly had a dolly"* they might omit "sick, sick, sick" and instead mime lying down and sleeping; then "quick, quick, quick" might become a running motion, "and his hat" could be mimed, and so could "rat! tat! tat!"

Then get them to reverse the process and "think" the whole song, but <u>sing</u> "sick, sick, sick", "quick, quick, quick" and so on, with or without the actions. The repertoire suggestions contain a number of songs that could be treated similarly.

Once this idea is firmly established, begin asking them to sign their little phrases without singing. Later, ask them to "think" the phrases, or "think" notated songs they already know, or even "think" brand-new phrases, before attempting to sign and/or sing them. It is a good idea before singing any song to make them close their eyes briefly, and "think" the first few notes before opening their eyes and starting to sing. This process of "internalising" the sound first will improve their pitching a lot. *Banana Splits*, mentioned in the section below, contains an excellent game with flash cards to encourage the "thinking voice".

Repertoire for younger children

- *Okki-tokki-unga, Apusskidu, Ta-ra-ra boom-de-ay, Flying a round* and several other compilations from publishers A&C Black are the "bench-mark" resources of songs for younger children. No first school music teacher should be without them.

- *Sing for Pleasure Junior Song Books*. There are ten of these, each with six or seven songs. They are cheap, and the songs are varied and entertaining. There is ample opportunity for movement, rounds, ostinati, elementary part-singing, musical games and experimentation, and all have been tried and tested in schools. The need for u   accompaniment is minimal in many cases, and if you can't read music yourself (shame on you!) you can learn most of the songs from the cassettes available. Highly recommended - these books could be all you ever need for first school singing! Book 1 *"Boom Chicka Boom"*, Book 2 *"Kumala Vista"*, Book 3 *"Tongo"*, Book 4 *"Popocatepetl"*, Book 5 *"Tall Straw Hat"*, Book 6 *"Rock'n'Roll"*, Book 7 *"Lost in Space"*, Book 8 *"I'm Gonna Sing"*, Book 9 *"Ghosts"*, Book 10 *"Bear Hunt"*

- .... also *"Sing a Part 1"* and *"Sing a Part 2"*. All available from Sing for Pleasure, Bolton Music Centre, New York, Bolton BL3 4NG, UK. Website www.singforpleasure.org.uk/catalog/

- *"Don't forget to feed it!"* and *"A Clang and a Clatter"* by Alan Simmons Highly entertaining and varied songs and rounds, some with accompaniment and some without. Alan Simmons Music, www.alansimmonsmusic.com/schools.php

- *"Growing with Music"* by Stocks and Maddocks, available from the Voices Foundation at www.voices.org.uk/growingwithmusic/

- *"If you ever meet a dinosaur"* by Camilla During. 20 varied songs for young children (including one with the marvellous title *"Can you eat your Teddy Bear?"*) which offer opportunities for improvisation and musical games but do need a piano accompanist. Available from publishers Boosey and Hawkes.

- *"Songs of England"*, *"Songs of Ireland"*, *"Songs of Scotland"*, *"Songs of Wales"*, *"Songs of Christmas"* and *"Songs of the Americas"*. One would probably not use these traditional tunes (some in foreign languages) every week, but an excellent resource when looking for that special song for a particular occasion. Suitable for slightly older children (say, 8 or 9 upwards), and they do need an accompanist. Available from publishers Boosey and Hawkes.

- *"Songbirds: Seasons"* and *"Songbirds: Me"* by Ana Sanderson and Marie Tomlinson. Each book has more than 20 songs with extensive and helpful notes on how to teach them and some ideas on extension activities. No piano accompaniment (guitar chords are given, though) but the CD included has instrumental tracks you can sing along to. Available from A&C Black. Intended for 4 - 7 year olds.

- *"Sing a silver lining"* by Jane Sebba. For slightly older children, a cheerful collection of songs like *"Whistle while you work"*, *"Zip-a-dee-doo-dah"* and *"The bare necessities"* with fairly simple piano accompaniments. Available from A&C Black.

- *"Banana Splits"* by Ana Sanderson. Really excellent varied material to lead children gently into part-singing. Lots of suggestions for movement and games, teaching notes, rounds, canons, second parts, some with accompaniment and some without - even advice about photocopying. Very highly recommended indeed. CD available. A&C Black.

- *"Michael Finnigin, tap your chinigin"* by Sue Nicholls, *"Tom Thumb's Musical Maths"* by Helen MacGregor and *"Bingo Lingo"* also by Helen MacGregor, all from A&C Black. Three books that link singing with other activities. *"Michael Finnigin"* contains a number of songs and games to provide easy ways into percussion and other instrumental work, improvisation etc. *"Tom Thumb"* has lots of songs that link music with counting, shapes, arithmetic etc. *"Bingo Lingo"* has songs, rhymes, chants and tongue twisters - *"... sing a song and rap a rhyme for language development and literacy ...."*!   All excellent.

- *"150 rounds for singing and teaching"* by Bolkovac and Johnson. Personally I don't like them but many people find rounds are an easy way to get into part-singing and develop pupils' confidence in their own ability to hold a line. This collection certainly offers a wealth of material to choose from, with a helpful index broken into various categories to help you select the most appropriate for your own needs. Available from Boosey and Hawkes.

Are you getting anywhere?

Despite modern education's obsession with recording and assessing, this is not meant to be an "end-of-term test" for your children, but a check-list to help you decide whether your efforts are being successful. So, at the end of their first couple of years with you, can your pupils ....

- sing a number of songs with reasonable accuracy, from memory, and with enjoyment? Do they have particular favourites? If not, are you choosing the right material for them?
- sing one or two songs with actions? Can they leave some of the music out and "think" it instead, just doing the actions?
- do some other musical games like the ones in, for instance, *"Banana Splits"* or *"Okki-tokki-unga"* or the *Sing for Pleasure Junior Song Books*?
- use the notes middle C up to A or B in their chest voices freely and without strain?
- sing some notes above C' using their head voices (think of Mrs.Butcher)?
- copy you when you sing and sign four- or five-note phrases to them?
- recognise four- or five-note phrases they already know, when you just sign them?
- recognise four or five note phrases they already know, when you show them the written notation?
- answer you with reasonable accuracy and confidence when you sing the register to them?
- and do they regard singing as a natural and normal thing to do, without reticence or embarrassment?

And at by the age of 9 or 10 can they ....

- sing even more songs accurately, from memory, and with enjoyment? Do you know which ones they like best?
- sing a few songs from written music, without burying their heads in the copies all the time? Have they practised using the written music just as a reminder, not something to hide behind?
- sing in more than one part, either in the form of a round, or a song with ostinato accompaniments, or even two distinct parts?
- use the range of notes from middle C up to top E or F with reasonable ease and without strain, using their head voices when necessary?
- copy you when you sing and sign six- or seven-note phrases to them?
- recognise longer phrases they already know, when you just sign them?
- recognise the same phrases from written notation?
- when presented with a new song or phrase in written notation, make a reasonable stab at "thinking" how it might sound?
- and do they still regard singing as a natural and normal thing to do? Can they sing in public (either in front of their friends or parents) confidently and with enjoyment?

If the answer to more than, say, two-thirds of these is "yes", then you're doing very well. If you can answer "yes" to ALL of them, well .... I'm very impressed. Buy yourself a present!

The next step

Much of what follows can be made to apply not just to your school choir, church choir or youth choir, but also to class singing in school, especially if your early efforts have been successful and your pupils can already sing confidently and joyfully. If you can look objectively at your oldest classes and answer "yes" to most of the check-list, you've already got a choir in all but name. However, for most successful teachers of singing who have established in their schools a régime in which singing is an integral and lively part of school life, the next and most natural step is to start an extra-curricular school choir to cater especially for those children who show the most aptitude and enthusiasm - and of course the more important of these two is enthusiasm; although you can teach them how to sing better, you can't do it if they don't want to learn.

Summary

- *Every child <u>can</u> sing and every child <u>should</u> sing*

- *Never make an issue of singing "right" or "wrong". There is no such thing as a "tone-deaf" child*

- *To open up the head voice, think of "Mrs.Butcher". Never approach it from below*

- *You will teach best what you know best*

- *Learn to value repetition - good songs are repetitive and good learning is repetitive*

- *Make singing a matter of daily routine*

- *"Signing" works really well, and is worth the trouble it takes to learn*

- *Notation is easy to teach and learn so long as you use it for its proper purpose and don't make it something it's not. It is not factual knowledge and it's not a mathematical exercise. It's a musical tool, an "aide memoire", and nothing more*

INTRODUCTION - SETTING UP YOUR CHOIR

Why do we run children's choirs?

The fact that you are reading this book means that you've probably decided what you think about this already. Suffice it to say, therefore (in case you ever have to justify yourself to a parent or head teacher, for instance), that singing lies at the root of nearly all world music, that virtually all peoples, tribes and races sing as soon as they can talk, that choral singing in the Western tradition is the best possible musical training, that there is no better way to develop aural and musical intelligence, that it demands a degree of teamwork that would make Manchester United look like a hockey match at St.Trinian's, and that it can make the freshest, liveliest, saddest, happiest, most soulful and altogether most beautiful sound on God's earth.

Luckily, children actually enjoy it as well.

As a choir-trainer your job is simple. You first have to attract children to your choir, and then keep them there. This means that your rehearsals must be interesting, your personality attractive, and that you must treat individual singers fairly and with respect. If you fail in these goals, they will vote with their feet.

So long as they are there, it is also your job to empower them - to show them how to make the very best of their natural ability, how to apply their intelligence to a simple function in order to transform it into high art, and how to nurture and enhance that intelligence. You will show them how to recognise when they are succeeding, and how to approach success calmly and constructively. You will show them how to recognise when they have failed, and how to utilise simple techniques to turn that failure back to success again. You will help them achieve what they will recognise and remember all their lives, as something joyous and very special.

And what do you get out of this?

Not a lot. There's certainly no money in it! But a successful choir *will* give you their loyalty, their affection, quite a lot of fun and the satisfaction of creating music so gorgeous it makes you cry. Nothing much, really ......

Adults and children

From the conductor's point of view children's and youth choirs are often more satisfactory to work with than choirs of adults. Nor should you assume that adults will necessarily be able to give you higher standards. Children are quick to learn and infinitely more flexible, able to absorb changes of style and method and a variety of repertoire that adults would find hard to cope with. Adults tend to have more entrenched opinions about what they want to sing, who they want to sit next to (or, frequently, who they don't want to sit next to), how they should learn the work etc., while children trust you to make the decisions. They have amazingly catholic tastes and will cheerfully tackle anything from Thomas Tallis to modern pop songs without complaint - provided that both are presented in a lively manner and are within their range of ability.

The question of trust is paramount. The most frustrating thing about training an adult choir is their insistence that they must feel absolutely secure about every single note - they do worry so! Almost every rehearsal can be punctuated by requests to "... just go over this particular bit of the tenor part once more, as we are not quite sure about the E flat at the end of the second bar?" Children, on the other hand, will be quite prepared to let such a detail slide if you tell them it's all right - they trust you. One of my colleagues has been heard to say that if he told his youth orchestra their next concert was at the top of Mount Everest, they'd just shrug and say "OK, when does the bus leave?"

This puts more responsibility on you, of course. If your choir fail to learn a particular piece in time for the next concert, it won't be their fault, but yours. If they perform badly it will be because you failed to pace their work, or made a foolish decision about the timing or the venue or something. If they have to sing to an empty building, it will be because your judgement was poor when you selected the venue, date or time for the concert, or because you failed to identify and target a suitable audience.

And you have to look after them all the time. You have to judge how tired or bored they are and tailor the rehearsal to suit, you must make sure that you can cope with little accidents and emergencies, you must ensure that your travel arrangements are foolproof, and at all times you must accept responsibility for their safety. For instance, at the end of rehearsal it is up to you to make sure they have all been collected by their parents and to wait behind until the last one has safely departed. The thought of some poor mite waiting fearfully in the dark long after the hall has been locked and bolted is too awful to contemplate, and it's just as much your responsibility as the musical decision making.

This means considering how many assistants you should have. Local Education Authorities have guidelines that apply to activities under their control, and even if you are running an independent choir you could find out what these are and follow them for your own protection as much as anything else. For example, the Authority I used to work for insisted that for any residential course or foreign trip, there should be one member of staff (or parent or other responsible adult - not necessarily a teacher) to every ten children, which was a good rule; I followed it when I started my own independent choirs, even though I didn't strictly have to.

Education Authorities are also bound by law to make sure that nobody gains access to young people who has a criminal record of offences against children, and UK law now stipulates child protection procedures for all organisations, whoever runs them. You need to check your legal responsibilities carefully. Get in touch with the relevant department at your local council, who should be able to advise you.

For the average weekly rehearsal, a main priority is to know that you can cope with an emergency. If one of the children is taken ill, is there someone else in the building who can help them or keep an eye on the rest of the choir while you do it yourself? If you are a man, is there an adult lady nearby in case one of the girls has a problem of an intimate nature? If you yourself were suddenly taken ill during rehearsal, do the children know where to go for help? One of the most effective ways of dealing with these requirements is to enlist the help of parents, who will instantly see the problem if you explain it to them in these terms. A rota system can make it very easy to have one or two parents sitting in the rehearsal or nearby just in case. They will probably be anxious to help in other ways, as well - marking the register, acting as choir librarian, organising drinks during the break etc.

Your rehearsal schedule

There is no doubt in my mind that if I could rehearse any of my choirs for, say, three hours every day, there is almost no limit to the standard they could achieve. This is pie in the sky, however, unless you work in a cathedral choir-school or are the Director of the Vienna Boys' Choir. It would probably be over-ambitious even then. For most of us a lengthy rehearsal once a week is the norm, although a school choir might manage shorter meetings more frequently.

Children can cope with more work than they are often given credit for. My younger choirs, with girls aged 8 to 13, meet once a week in the evening for an hour and a half. We have a break in the middle of five minutes or so. My older choir, aged 11 to 18, meets for a whole day once every three or four weeks in term time, but during the school holidays we rehearse for three or four days at a time, eight or more hours a day, in blocks of 90 to 120 minutes. Sessions are longer in the morning, and get shorter as the day wears on and concentration wanes. They cope with this work-load very well.

One does, of course, have to think about the danger of over-tiring voices. It is normal and healthy for the muscles around the mouth, throat and larynx to feel a little tired after a long session. But if overworking is causing actual

25

trauma, the symptom is the need to keep coughing because delicate tissues are becoming irritated and inflamed, and you should think of stopping. If you have trained your singers to produce their sound in a relaxed manner this is rarely a problem. Do encourage them to bring bottles of water into the rehearsal. Singing dries the membranes of mouth and throat.

To rehearse for these lengths of time it is essential to plan your work and vary the activity frequently. Move from a classical piece to a modern one, spend time note-bashing something they don't know yet, then go on to polish up something they have already learned, then spend ten minutes working on some aspect of vocal technique etc.

It's a good idea to do the detailed work earlier on, while their concentration is good and their brains are fresh. Later move to the "rough-hewn" work of learning new songs. This is the opposite of the advice one is normally given, but it works for me. And always finish a session by singing something (not necessarily the whole song, but a short section at least) they know well and enjoy, so they leave rehearsal with a sense of accomplishment.

Tick each song off on a grid as you rehearse it, so that halfway through the term you can look and see "Oh yes, I've done that one four times already, but this one we've only looked at twice". This is good advice whether or not you have the luxury of ample rehearsal time.

How many parts should you sing in?

Every young choir should sing in unison sometimes, with at least one unison work in every programme. Handel is good. Have a look at *Shine out, great sun* from *Samson,* or *Where'er you walk.* Wide range, lots of big leaps to navigate, lovely tunes, and not often performed by children so you're doing something a bit special.

You have a responsibility to your members not to let them become entrenched in just one part, but to continue using their whole voice.

For instance, very few young "altos" are really altos at all - they are mostly sopranos who have chosen to concentrate on the lower part of their voice. Sadly, more do so from laziness or shyness than from real physical necessity. You would be failing if you did not make sure that they still had a soprano voice at the end of their time with you, and to have it they must use it. Therefore, I make all my young singers do their warm-ups together, and I insist that everyone shall sing in the same keys and throughout the same range at least some of the time. Consequently, we have an alto section who can all sing up to top G above the treble stave - and sopranos who can reach G below middle C. Yes, really!

By the same token, do some two-part work and don't allow your singers to be too rigid about which part they sing. It's a good idea sometimes to swap the parts over. My younger choirs include in their repertoires Bob Chilcott's *Two Singing Songs*. These excellent pieces are interestingly dissonant, totally charming and really very easy. We don't know who is singing which part until just before each concert, as we line up in the dressing-room and number ourselves: "You're 1, you're 2, you're 1, you're 2, and you're 1, and 2, and 1, 2, 1, 2, 1 .... now, in the *Two Singing Songs*, all the "ones" sing the lower part, and all the "twos" sing the top part. And swap over for the second song!" It's a good introduction to the art of singing "scrambled", of which more anon.

Fortunately there is no shortage of repertoire for upper voice choirs, whether you wish to sing in unison, two or three parts or even more. Therefore it is easy to find enough material for the younger choir that needs to sing in unison or two parts most of the time. Don't be afraid to do this. A really good performance in only two parts is much better than a ropy one in three, so cut your coat according to your cloth. Of course, the bulk of upper-voice material tends to be in three parts, and here you must consider the question of balance .....

Balance

Most children want to sing the top part ("first soprano") because they find it easier. That alone is a good reason for not letting them do it, but making them <u>all</u> learn <u>all</u> the parts. Their musicianship and their awareness of the harmonic basis of the music will improve if you can make them swap parts readily.

In a two-part choir you need more singers on the lower part than the upper (well, it stands to reason, doesn't it? Higher sounds are more penetrating). Similarly, when in three parts you need most singers in the second sopranos. The second soprano section is the "power-house" of the choir. The altos provide the bedrock on which the harmony sits, while the first sopranos are the icing on the cake, so to speak.

Try to have a balance of power and experience in each part – especially don't allow all the best singers to congregate in the firsts. Explain to them that every part must have its own balance of strength and ability, and every part is equally important. I usually put new members into the second sopranos, and only move them either up or down when they have gained experience at reading and singing an inner part, and I have had an opportunity to assess where they will be most useful.

In our older choir last season we had 16 first sopranos, 30 second sopranos and 15 altos, and we felt the balance was exactly right.

Choosing your singers

Why bother?

For years I conducted two girls' choirs, one a highly selective choir which auditioned prospective members because there were so many applicants that we didn't have room for them all, the other was completely non-selective - any girl who wished to join could do so. True, the selective one was better (though to be fair they were much older) but really the difference was not so very great - certainly not great enough to justify being selective if you don't need or wish to be.

In the non-selective one we never had to ask a girl to leave because she couldn't cope. We certainly had one or two who sang out of tune, or wandered around a bit when singing in parts, but in every case they quickly got the hang of it and became useful members.

Consequently when I moved on and started my own organisation, Harmony Girls' Choirs with two training choirs, main choir and chamber choir, I made the deliberate decision not to audition and never had cause to regret it. Chanterelles, the very large and very fine girls' choir that came second in the 2000 Sainsbury's "Choir of the Year" contest, did not select its singers in any way. If they can do it, so can we.

It's really a question of rehearsal technique and common-sense. A child with an inaccurate ear who sits every week between two big, strong, accurate singers, can't really do anything but improve! The warm-up routine also helps to give them the knack of listening to and controlling their voices. Inaccurate singing is often not a question of being unable to hear what sound they <u>should</u> be making, but of being unable to control the voice and listen to it simultaneously. In other words, it's not a physiological or intellectual failing, but simply a lack of choral technique ..... and <u>that</u> can be taught.

One of the really lovely things about young choirs is that, provided they are being run and rehearsed well, they almost never get <u>worse</u>. Every year some of your most experienced singers move on, and you think "Oh my goodness, we're going to be in real trouble next season - all the best singers have left!" And yet, year on year, standards nearly always improve. The reason is twofold. First, though your most senior singers have left, the next cohort have been steadily getting stronger all this time without you noticing - they were being overshadowed by the seniors. Now they <u>are</u> the seniors. Second, although each year you take in some more beginners and need in a sense to train and establish the choir all over again, each year the base from which you start is a little better, and you will reach "performance level" that much sooner.

If you DO decide to audition your singers after all, by all means let them sing a prepared piece so they can start from a position of confidence, but this is not the most important thing. Really your priorities should be ...

(a) control of the voice. <u>Can they make their voice do what they want</u>? Make them sing a scale, up and down - sometimes you come across a child who finds it hard to start at the top of a scale and come down, because no one has ever made them do it before. Can they swoop or slide from the bottom of their voice to the top and back? Can they sing a scale or arpeggio to different words (try "tickety-boo" or "cucumber" on each note)? They may find these hard to do because of unfamiliarity, but if they seem to pick up the idea quickly, there isn't going to be a problem, is there?

(b) aural perception. <u>Can they hear what they need to hear</u> in order to sing in your choir? Can they sing both notes of a two-note chord? Give them plenty of time to try this, they may never have done it before. If they quickly get the hang of it, no problem. You are looking for potential, not experience. Then try a three-note chord. Can they imitate you when you sing a phrase to them? Can they sing the same phrase while you play something else on the piano? Or, more difficult, while you sing a harmony part? Can they sing something really easy like *"Three Blind Mice"* while you play *"God Save the Queen"* to put them off? Or, hardest of all, can they sing *"Three Blind Mice"* in one key while you play it in another? If they can, this means they have the ability, so vital to good part-singing, to hear and control their own sound despite distractions.

(c) <u>music reading and speed of learning</u>. The purpose of music reading is to speed the process of learning and to help them remember what they have already learnt. You are never going to perform anything without rehearsing it first, so perfect sight-singing is a luxury. But it is important to see that they can make sense of a vocal score, know which part to follow and where it has disappeared to when they turn the page, and can follow the "shape" of the written music. Give them a simple part-song they have never seen before, and sing them the first page or so while they point to the music. Then have them sing it with you, and then on their own (without the words if they prefer). Gradually give them less and less support from the piano, and start to emphasise the other parts more. Finally stop playing their part completely, and if they are still singing <u>roughly</u> the right thing by the bottom of the page, that's good enough. This may sound slap-dash but my selective choir were chosen like this, and they were known to learn a major choral work (Verdi *Requiem* or Carl Orff *Carmina Burana* for example) in two days flat. What more could I ask? What more did I need?

(d) <u>voice quality - the last and least important criterion</u>. Look carefully at any candidates with great big "stagey" voices, or those who habitually force or sing out of tune, as these have the potential to damage your choir's sound. But children with little weedy voices, or even voices that just aren't very nice, are not a problem if they meet the other criteria. The same can apply to children who try to use their chest voices all the time, provided you know they <u>can</u> get into their head voice a little bit. Once they've done your warm-up routine for a few weeks they'll probably be changed out of all recognition. You're not looking for children who are good singers. You're looking for potential. <u>You</u> are going to turn them into good singers.

Boys versus girls

If you are running a choir in a mixed school you may not have any choice, but if you are in a situation where you can choose whether to run a boys' choir, a girls' choir or a mixed choir, you do have to consider the differences between them.

This may be an unpopular view, but I think a really good young boys' choir beats a really good young girls' choir hands down. The flip side is that there aren't many really good boys' choirs - good girls' and mixed choirs are much more common. Also, as the girls get older they quickly gain the edge for the obvious reason that they can keep singing and learning without the colossal disruption boys experience at the onset of puberty.

In the young mixed choir the boys can often be stronger but may also be less accurate as the physiology of their voices seems to make them harder to control. They can sometimes overwhelm the girls, who tend to be more flexible and subtle. Nevertheless many choir trainers run mixed choirs with tremendous success, and they are right to do so, for adult choirs need a supply of men to fill the tenor and bass sections. There is greater resistance and negative peer pressure about singing among boys, so we should all do what we can to encourage boys to sing and keep singing. An alternative and equally successful strategy is to keep the sexes separate, so the boys feel that singing is a normal thing for them to do, not something their friends might label "girly".

If you run a young mixed choir you have to face the problem of what to do with the boys when their changing voices make it difficult or impossible for them to continue. You can defer this decision for a long time by letting them sing alto which they often do very well, but in the end you will have to decide. Do you make them leave, or do you start a tenor/baritone/bass section for them?

To make them leave seems harsh. To allow them to stay means having a section that cannot work to the same standard as the rest of the choir because for some time the boys' range will be limited. They will probably not be true tenors or basses for ages, but will have a restricted baritone range running from about middle C downwards for an octave or so. This in turn means choosing (or writing or arranging) music for a rather non-standard type of choral ensemble, so that the tail will be wagging the dog.

In some situations - school choirs, in particular - a highly effective solution is to "bump" the immature tenors and basses by getting members of staff and parents to sing with them. This is ideal, for it enables you to operate a full four-part choir without compromising standards, and allows the young men to learn the craft and skill of singing tenor and bass in a protected environment where their limited range will not be an embarrassment to them.

It is rare to find a four-part school or youth choir that does not need to adopt this strategy and bring in men from outside. However, I would be very unfair if I did not say that there <u>are</u> choir-trainers who have the skill or find themselves in a situation that enables them to fill their tenor and bass sections entirely with 16- to 19-year-olds. Where this works, it can work astonishingly well, for young men of this age have lively minds, a ready sense of humour, and can bring to the choir an energy that informs everything it sings. Few who heard them will forget Gillian Dibden's marvellous Berkshire Youth Choir in the Sainsbury's "Choir of the Year" competition some years ago.

Your Accompanist

Apart from you, the accompanist is the most important person in your choir. He or she can make or mar every performance. You need to consider the following ....

(a) You need a very good pianist indeed. To be quite honest, if you can only find one of the mums who got to Grade 5 fifteen years ago, you'd be better off playing yourself and directing from the piano, or training the choir to sing a completely unaccompanied repertoire. It can be done, even with the youngest. It just takes more time finding the right music.

(b) You need a pianist with the maturity and experience to be able to follow you and the choir whatever you do. They will have to reflect each shade and nuance, every *ritenuto* and *stringendo*. They will also need to be aware when the choir is rushing or dragging, and be able to help you control it. Sadly, young pianists are often not good at this sort of thing - they're too busy playing the notes.

(c) You need an accompanist who is not scared of playing strongly and firmly. A choir needs plenty of support. Many accompanists JUST DON'T PLAY LOUD ENOUGH.

(d) You need an accompanist with the ability to concentrate just as much as you do during rehearsals. Nothing is more annoying than the pianist who says "sorry, where are you going from?" just as you're about to start. Also, the ideal accompanist would be able to take over the choir if you were taken ill suddenly in the middle of a concert. It has happened.

I am fortunate in having several such wonderful musicians on whom I can call. However, I also have a theory that a really good young choir should be able to perform perfectly well without a conductor. After all, when you have a delightful choir of beautiful young ladies who sing like angels and know every note from memory, who needs some hairy old git prancing about and getting in the way? So I do frequently direct my younger choirs from the piano. It works, and we have done some nice concerts this way, but I am forced to admit that they sing better when I conduct them, and they seem to prefer it. So my theory is just that - a pretty theory rather than a demonstrable fact.

Choosing repertoire - where to look and what to look for

Most of the major publishers have good lists of music suitable for young choirs. The two that have made most of the running in recent years are Faber's and Boosey & Hawkes. Faber's have a number of excellent books - quite expensive but you get several songs in each - offering a variety of styles from Andrew Lloyd Webber to Schubert, *Godspell* to plainchant. Well worth a look.

Boosey & Hawkes have their Choral Experience Series, published in smart red leaflets and edited and compiled in America by Doreen Rao. This series is very mixed indeed. It contains many songs composed or arranged by American composers for the American market which will not appeal to British choir-trainers at all. Some of them are truly awful. On the other hand the list is so large that one is always bound to find something one likes, and there are a number of titles that really are enormously successful, including ...

- *Niska Banja* - seven beats in a bar, Serbian words, 4 parts and not nearly as hard as it sounds. Children and audiences love it.
- *A-tisket a-tasket* and *When I sing* - jazzy songs with "do-be-do-be-do" words, good fun.
- *Goin' up a-yonder* - nice gospel song with a big ending, sounds harder than it is.
- *She shall have music* - odd but very effective.
- *Las Amarillas* - Mexican style, audiences love it but <u>very</u> hard.
- *Cantate Domino* - a good way of approaching modern, partly aleatoric music; has an accompaniment for synthesizer but works perfectly well without it.

The one composer in the "Choral Music Experience" series who is always worth considering is Stephen Hatfield. Although he comes from Canada, he writes very effectively in ethnic styles from all over the world and has a wonderful understanding of just how much is possible for young singers. That is not to say his music is not difficult - it often is - but it is always achievable and produces impressive effects. As well as *Las Amarillas*, have a look at *Three ways to vacuum your house*, *Run children run*, *Ain't that news*, *La Lluvia* and the long, wonderfully impressive *African Celebration*.

There are several British composers and arrangers worth looking out for. John Rutter rarely puts a foot wrong, and his *For the beauty of the earth* is a great favourite of ours. Anything arranged by Gwynn Arch will be worth performing. My younger choir like his *Four Negro Spirituals* very much. John Gardner is often subtle and amusing, and his *Waly waly* is a little masterpiece, though hard to bring off. Michael Neaum and Bob Chilcott are both gifted writers for young voices - Chilcott's *Can you hear me?* complete with deaf signing is a real show-stopper, and children love doing it. Neaum's *Sakura* is incredibly atmospheric, but is really easy to do despite being in four parts and in Japanese!

If you are looking for unison songs I particularly recommend Richard Rodney Bennett's *The Aviary* and *The Insect World*. These are two exquisitely crafted song cycles, full of subtlety, humour and good tunes that can be sung with profit by children of most ages from 10 or so upwards. You need a good pianist, though.

Britten has left us many wonderful things including the *Missa Brevis* (needs an organ and is very hard, but <u>what</u> a powerful piece!), the well-known *Ceremony of Carols* (also difficult, and needs a harpist or a good pianist) and *Friday Afternoons* (easy songs for younger children). Both Britten and Bennett seem to have that wonderful knack of writing so that whatever comes next always lies comfortably in wherever the voice happens to be at the time!

If you are running a young church choir, have a look at *High Praise*, a book of anthems for upper-voice choirs edited by Barry Rose (Novello). This has some nice things in it most, though not all, from the 20th Century, with performance notes for each piece.

One other composer I must mention is Alan Simmons, whose amusing collections *Don't forget to feed it* and *A clang and a clatter* include well-crafted little songs and rounds for the classroom or the younger choir. *Butterfly* and *Lost in Space* are our favourites. Alan Simmons also publishes sheet music for older choirs - *Harry* by Catherine Howe and Alan's own *All you were and all you are* are charming, and popular with singers and audiences.

Finally, forgive me if I mention some music I've written myself. *Silly Songs for Kids* is suitable for younger choirs, not at all "politically correct" (titles include *Fat Man Shout* and *Lavatory Song*) but children love them. *Stone in the Water* is for the good school choir, and *Twelve o'clock Stone* for the more advanced upper-voice choir, while *Four Corners of the Building* is difficult, suitable only for the most proficient youth choir, but unusual and very atmospheric and beautiful - but I suppose I <u>would</u> say that, wouldn't I? These titles are available from The Choirmaster Press (www.choirmaster.co.uk).

When assessing material, look carefully at the alto part. Inevitably, to keep the upper parts within a comfortable range arrangers often find themselves writing alto parts that are very low - too low for young singers, in some cases. While the odd bottom G or even F is manageable, if they occur too often the song is best avoided. This is particularly true with unaccompanied songs. Most choirs go flat sometimes when singing *a capella*, and when this happens the poor altos can suddenly find themselves falling out of the bottom of their voices! The answer is not to go flat, of course, and there are ways of avoiding this, but it is a danger to be considered in advance.

Many choir-trainers become adept at composing or making arrangements for their choirs to use. This is not the place to embark on a lengthy dissertation on writing music for choirs, but it is the place to say a few words about copyright. If you compose a completely original song for your choir then it is your own property - you own the copyright. You have make sure you can prove that you wrote the song on such and such a date, in case somebody else tries to steal it. Traditionally there are two methods of doing this. One is to seal a copy in an envelope and post it to yourself preferably by registered mail. When it arrives, keep it unopened. The second is to have a couple of copies signed and dated by someone reputable (bank manager, vicar, head teacher etc.) and keep those safely so that if there is ever any question of the song's provenance you have some tangible evidence. Of course, you need to be sure that you have used words that are "in the public domain". Poetry written in the last seventy years is usually copyright in which case you may not use it without obtaining permission from the copyright owner - probably the publisher of the book you got it from.

Arranging existing music is fraught with difficulties. To put it very simply (and this is indeed a gross simplification) until the composer has been dead for seventy years his music is copyright and you may not make a written arrangement of it without permission. Copyright owners - usually music publishers - will often give you permission to arrange their songs if you write and ask, especially if you offer (a) to use the arrangement only in performances by your own choir, and (b) not to sell or disseminate any copies outside the choir. Sometimes this permission may be given free of charge, and sometimes you have to pay. For instance I recently paid a publisher £47 for permission to make and use an arrangement of a Cole Porter song, which for a big choir is not an unreasonable investment although there is also the cost of photcopying to be considered.

Often it's hard to find out who the copyright owner is. I recommend that you purchase a copy of the *Music Education Yearbook* and/or the *Music Yearbook*, both published by Rhinegold. Here you will find a host of useful information including names and addresses of music publishers, and of the Performing Right Society, the Mechanical Copyright Protection Society and the Music Publishers' Association. I have found the last one to be extremely helpful in questions of copyright ownership, and they also publish a useful booklet on the rules of copyright which you should certainly obtain and study - it's free.

On the internet the UK Copyright Service have a useful summary at "www.copyrightservice.co.uk/protect/p07_music_copyright".

You are very unlikely to be given permission to arrange music by modern "serious" composers, so your version of Benjamin Britten's *Ceremony of Carols* for sopranos, baritone solo, piano, ocarina and Japanese nose-flute is probably out of the question. Older composers are fair game, however.

Take Handel, for example. His music itself, and the words, are "in the public domain" because he's been dead so long. You may make whatever arrangements and alterations you see fit without asking anyone. You can even publish them (i.e. make copies and lend or sell them) if you wish. However, a copyright may still exist on a publisher's <u>edition</u> of Handel's music. This means that if Boosey & Hawkes published their own edition of, say, the *Messiah* (they don't, actually) you must not photocopy parts of it for your choir to use - the printed image is their property and they own the copyright on it. This ought to be obvious. They paid for the editing, layout and printing so they are entitled to make from it any money there is to be made. If you wanted to use their edition, you should have bought it - anything else is cheating and illegal. If we don't play fair by the publishers in this respect, in the long run we will be the losers because they will find it uneconomic to publish the music we want to use. They have a living to make, too.

If, however, you create your own edition of *Messiah* with your own editorial content, your own layout and perhaps your own special arrangement of the parts to make it more suitable for your own singers, and produce your own printed version by writing it out or printing it from a computer, then the copyright in that edition is yours - no problem. There is nothing to stop you using the Boosey & Hawkes edition as your source, either. They may own the printed image, but they have no claim over Handel's crotchets and quavers (unless, that is, their own editor has added some, which is possible; he should have made this clear in the text though).

Music desktop publishing is a great boon for people like us, and many choir-trainers use it to produce good-looking and easy-to-read arrangements and editions of "public domain" composers for their choirs to sing. Two of the best programmes are "Coda Finale" from America (very effective but quite hard to learn. It took me nine or ten years to use it effectively and fluently, but then I was very loyal to it). "Sibelius" is British, more expensive to buy, much easier to use, very fast and beautiful to read. It is used by some commercial publishers, but is less flexible than "Coda Finale".

I use both. For simple music I prefer Sibelius, but for really complicated stuff I still like an old version of Finale. Beware: once you get started on this sort of thing, you'll never break free of it. Computers seem to suck you in, and you can waste an awful lot of time just fiddling around if you're not careful.

There are two other "rights" you need to be aware of. One is the Mechanical Copyright - the right to make recordings and broadcasts of published works. These normally belong to the publisher. If you are lucky enough to be invited to sing on the radio, for instance, the owners of the mechanical copyright are entitled to a small payment. Fortunately the radio station will usually take care of this. If you want to make a tape recording of your choir to sell to parents or at concerts, you don't need to ask permission beforehand except in the case of new works that have never been recorded before, but there will probably be a small fee to pay and you should contact the Mechanical Copyright Protection Society and ask them what to do. They're very helpful. Find their address in the *Music Yearbook*.

Performing Right is a bit more complicated. The copyright owner (sometimes the composer, sometimes the publisher) is entitled to a payment whenever his or her piece is performed. In most cases this is collected by the Performing Right Society whose advice you should seek and follow - you'll find them both helpful and very reasonable (once again, see the *Yearbook* for an address). In larger concert-halls the management may get you to fill in a form for the Performing Right Society, or you can send the Society a copy of the concert programme so they know what you've done. Frequently with our kind of music the pieces are so short and the profits to be made from our concerts are so small that you may not even hear from them.

However, be very wary about performing stage musicals, or extracts from stage musicals. The performing right for these lies normally with the publishers, not the Performing Right Society, and they are very jealous of their rights. You must seek permission from them for every performance, and they will often ask for a fairly stiff fee. They may want to know the status of your performers (amateur, professional, students etc.), the size of the hall and the cost of the tickets. One is very well aware that up and down the country many school performances of musicals like *Oliver, Grease, Fiddler on the Roof, Annie* etc. are completely illegal, and sooner or later a school is going to find itself in hot water for bucking the system - and quite right, too. Why should we have free and unrestricted use of intellectual property that has taken months and even years of a composer's life and effort to produce? This also applies to operas and other "staged" works like Britten's *Noye's Fludde*.

Summary

- *Children trust you. Can you be trusted? Will you look after them both musically and personally?*

- *Children can do more work than we give them credit for, but you must PLAN*

- *In part-singing, the highest part should be the weakest*

- *Choosing your singers - why bother?*

- *Single-sex choirs may be the easy way out, but sometimes that's the best way to take*

- *If you can't get a really good accompanist, do without*

- *Be sure you understand the rules about copyright - they are not as restrictive as you might think*

EXPOSITION - YOUR CHOIR IN REHEARSAL

Warm-up exercises

The "choir warm-up" is far and away the most important part of every rehearsal (and every performance, don't forget), and should never be omitted. It is important because ....

- ... it establishes a routine for every rehearsal, and young people like routine because it makes them feel secure .....

- ... it helps them to concentrate on the job in hand, and put aside all the little distractions they bring with them to the rehearsal room .....

- ... it brings that all-important feeling of teamwork and togetherness ....

- ... it encourages young singers to feel that they are working in a professional way .....

- ... it makes them feel special. That's why they like doing it. They will say they don't, but believe me, they do really! All the other performers in the concert are just sitting around waiting for the show to begin - it is only the <u>choir</u> that have to do this special thing, because they are <u>special people</u>! I often find an opportunity to do it in public for precisely this reason. Our older choir which undertakes a foreign tour every year has warmed-up in a beautiful botanical garden at the university in Budapest, in village squares in France, under some railway arches in Prague, in the corner of a field and in motorway service-stations on the way to destinations all over Europe, as well as in peaceful English churchyards and even in the street ....

- ... and, most important of all, because this is where your real voice-training takes place. It is these simple and repetitive exercises that help young singers to use their natural God-given voices without the distraction of words, tunes, harmonies and dynamics. This is their chance to think about where the breath comes from, where the focus of the voice is (and it can, and should, move around while they sing), what their voice sounds like and how they can influence it. This is the chance to develop the rather impressive range of which the young voice is capable.

So here is ....

"THE FAMOUS SEVEN-STEP WARM-UP"

ONE

Begin by breathing. Ensure that your choir are quiet, have discarded their chewing-gum, left their music on the floor out of harm's way, finished their conversations and are standing properly (see the section on "Posture" later on). Then ask them to just breathe in and out slowly and silently for a minute or two - as long as their concentration will allow.

Then make them breathe in slowly while you count to eight (about *crotchet = 60*), keeping their shoulders relaxed and still. Hold the breath a moment, and then let it out slowly to another count of eight. Ask them how empty they are at the end. They should try to finish with the feeling that their lungs are still a third or even half-full. Now breathe in for a count of eight and out for a count of twelve. Then try eight and sixteen if you think they can manage it.

The object of this exercise - and <u>do</u> explain this to them - is firstly to concentrate the mind in the body; to make them forget all the distracting things they have been thinking about, and turn their attention inwards to the functioning of their voices. Secondly it is to help them develop control over their breathing, particularly over breathing out. Talk of "eking" the breath out little by little, always under control, and not letting it go with a "whoosh". If they find this hard, make them let it out in little sips - "sss .... sss .... sss ...".

Finally, make them do the same exercise while putting their finger-tips on their ribs high up, below the collar-bone. Make them feel their ribs rise while they breathe in. Then as they let the breath out in a slow controlled fashion, make them try to "hold" the ribs up with the fingers, as though the fingers were glued to the tops of their chests. They should feel their stomachs going in as their diaphragms work - they will end up with an "empty" feeling in their stomachs. Then let them do the same thing without the fingers. This "high ribs" idea will encourage a lovely erect posture.

TWO

Now we are all quietly concentrating, start to open up the voice. <u>Always open up the lower part of the voice first</u>, by singing this exercise ....

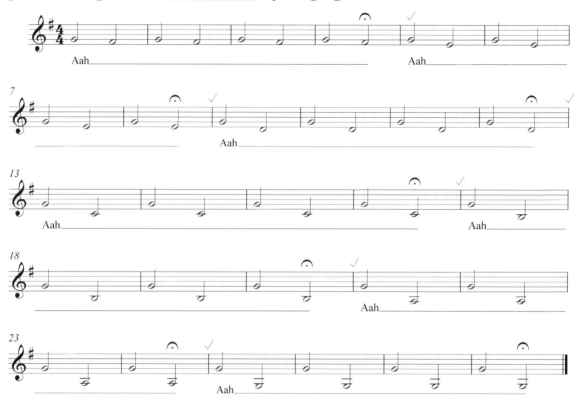

Make sure they are singing eight notes to a breath, controlling the breath so that they have enough left at the end of each phrase to "look after" the last note and not let it "droop" - it needs to be just a little longer than the other seven. Then take a gentle, fairly slow breath and start the next phrase.

As the phrases drop lower and lower, talk to them while they sing, encouraging them to think about where the sound is. Tell them to imagine that their voice is very heavy, and is just tumbling under its own weight loosely down into their chest or even into their tummy. Make them keep their mouths quite open and "wide" so they sing "aah" and not "er". Don't allow them to sing loudly - NONE of these exercises should be sung loudly - and tell them that if the notes are really too low and won't come out, just stop - it won't matter. These exercises are self-defeating if they involve very much effort.

Later on you will find that this exercise, particularly if you frequently remind them of it during rehearsals, will tend to develop a nice fat tone at the bottom of the voice which sounds natural and yet makes a wonderful contrast with the clear, powerful upper register we hope to achieve.

THREE

Now inject a little life into the proceedings by making them stretch, reaching up over their heads with both arms and feeling the tightness in their shoulders. Hold this stretch, and waggle all the fingers. Then allow just the fingers to flop down. Don't just tell them what to do, do it yourself in front of them. Now let the whole hand flop down from the wrist, and then flop the arm from the elbow. Then let the arms flop down by their sides.

Now flop the head forward onto the chest, and begin to slowly fold downwards from the waist until they reach a touch-your-toes position with the head and hands hanging down loosely. Then slowly unfold until they are standing upright again.

Now another big stretch, arms in the air. Make an eyes-wide smily face, and waggle the fingers again. Then hold the position but waggle the whole hands. Then waggle the head as well - tell them to really mess their hair up! At the same time make a "burble-burble" noise so that the mouth and lips are waggling too. Now waggle everything - hands, heads, mouths, knees, bottoms - the lot! Then relax and go straight into the next exercise.

FOUR

Now introduce "sirens". Ask them to sing the word "sing" on any old note. Then make it "sing-ng-ng-ng-ng". Now just sing the "ng-ng-ng-ng". That's what we call a "siren" - a sound made in the larynx with an open mouth (it's not the same as humming). It needs very little breath, and very little effort as virtually all the muscles of mouth and throat are in a relaxed state.

Now turn this into the sound of a police siren
with a "flick" in the top, like this .....

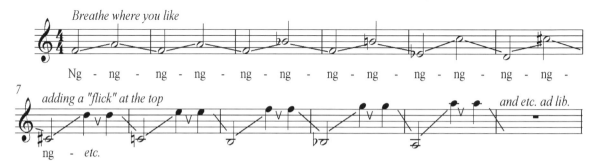

The pitches given are only approximate of course; gradually push the siren lower and higher, until they are going as high and as low as they can manage. Making open-mouthed chewing motions while doing it will look disgusting and might make them giggle, but helps them learn to keep the larynx and throat relaxed while thinking about some other kind of muscular action, as they eventually should do while articulating words.

Finally have them "siren" a well-known tune. We use *"My bonny lies over the ocean"* in an easy key like F major, and instead of chewing we articulate the words as well - just the vowel shapes and consonants, but keeping the basic "ng-ng-ng" throughout.

FIVE

Now you can work on the upper register, using this "octave exercise" ....

Don't allow the choir to breathe at the minim in the middle, although they'll naturally want to. Make them put a little crescendo on it to carry them over the top and down again.

Once again, let them think about the placing of the voice in the body - "chest, head, head, chest, chest, head he ... ead, head, chest, chest, head, head". Once they are familiar with it, encourage them to sing with the eyebrows and the chin: as the voice goes up the eyebrows go up, and the chin tucks in imperceptibly to avoid any hint of tightness in the throat.

Try this exercise in different keys. With use, you'll be surprised just how high you can take them without any strain. Even the key of F (top note B flat) should be no real effort, but as always let them stop singing or leave notes out rather than try too hard - everything should feel easy or it's useless.

Try singing this exercise in, say, the key of C major and stopping on the top note (F) and holding it. Then take them straight in on the top F, hold it, and imagine that they can "swallow" the sound, taking it back into their mouths, passing between the teeth and over the tongue towards the back of the head, getting smaller and smaller all the time. I mime this as they sing, taking my fingers slowly back past my mouth until I'm pointing at the back of my neck.

Then reverse it, starting the top F "right inside" and slowly bringing it out past the teeth and out in front of them. In time they will begin to develop a very fine control over the volume, and some may start to get the knack of a real *mezzo voce*. But don't describe it in terms of "loud" and "soft", only of "outside" and "inside".

SIX

Now an exercise with the face. Sing a scale of, say, D major one octave, up and down, to "Yah! Yah! Yah! Yah!" Make the "Y" sound as strong as possible, almost violent. Try doing this while actually singing quite softly, because as usual we don't want any of these exercises to involve anything like a *forte*. The purpose here is to work the muscles of the mouth and palate.

Then tell them to imagine that they have won a million pounds on the Lottery! Naturally, they are excited, shocked and very, very pleased! What we are after is an expression of delighted surprise, the mouth smiling and well open, the eyes wide, the eyebrows and cheekbones raised. Now sing "Yah! Yah! Yah!" with the same expression.

This "Lottery face" will stand them in good stead in all their singing. It brightens the tone and the vowel sounds - especially in words like "mild" and "smiling" which are very vulnerable to poor pronunciation. It is also remarkably difficult to sing flat with this facial expression, and I have known a young choir actually lift the pitch slightly in mid-phrase when I made this face at them.

As an extension to this exercise, sing arpeggios to "Yah! Yah! Yah!" as well. Make this a quick-fire contest - "Right! That was a scale of D major, so now sing an arpeggio of D major! Good! Now an arpeggio of D minor. OK, you've just finished on D, so now sing an E. Yes, that's it! So now sing an arpeggio of E major! ....." and so on.

Sing these arpeggios quite fast, and get them to speed up as they pass over the top. Then add the tenth as well before coming down, but make it quick. Then add the twelfth, too, going even quicker. Don't be too concerned about accuracy. Tell them to "take their voices by surprise". They enjoy this game, and provided they are moving fast enough so there is no time to put in a concentrated effort, can reach surprisingly high notes without straining.

SEVEN

Finally, repeat exercise 3 so they have something both physically active and relaxing before they start work on the actual musical rehearsal.

Always follow this routine without variation, so that they know exactly what is coming next. Do it at the beginning of every rehearsal, and before every performance. And whenever you are all together, start each day with the same routine, even if you have no rehearsals or concerts that day. On long coach journeys we will often work through the routine at rest stops, much to the amusement of the coach-drivers and the passing public.

If you feel that the higher notes are not coming out as freely and easily as they ought, try a couple of things to improve the "placing" of the voice and encourage your singers to "get on top of" their high notes instead of reaching up for them. The first is an old chestnut, "bella signora" sung to an arpeggio in various keys, with a really long and exaggerated "nnnyy" sound in the middle of "signora" which hopefully has the effect of connecting the sound (via the tongue, as it were) with the resonating sinus cavities above the mouth and behind the nose.

Second, when singing any exercise that involves high notes, an improved version of the old choir-trainer's "hole in the top of the head" idea. Have your choir sit on the edge of their chairs with their hands on their knees, looking fixedly at a point on the floor about a metre in front of them. Then make them sing the exercise while trying, without raising their eyes, to aim the sound up at you. I sometimes do this during normal rehearsal when we encounter a high passage that begins to sound strained. Singing it once or twice in this strange manner is usually enough to remind them to keep their chins down, throats relaxed, and heads full of sound.

Pacing your choir's work

There is a limit to the amount of improvement a young choir can achieve in any one piece of music, and one of the great skills of choir-training is the ability to recognise this and plan for it. If you know you have a performance in 6 weeks' time but the choir have reached their optimum preparation after four rehearsals, the last two weeks will be frustrating because they won't get any better however much work they do. There comes a point where children just can't absorb any more detail in a song. It's not their fault. The younger the children, the sooner they will peak. Once you realise that they have learned the song as thoroughly as they're going to, you can still sing it through each week to keep it "on the boil", but don't actually work on it needlessly - it'll get no better and could get worse.

How to teach a song

You will naturally tend to do this by example, and you will be right. They will learn the fastest if you sing to them rather than play on the piano. Begin phrase by phrase, making them copy each one in turn, but as they absorb the style and feeling of the song you can gradually increase the amount until they are copying two or three or even four phrases at a time.

Pretty early on, pick out any recurring motifs such as a repeated rhythm or a recurrent interval or pattern of notes, and draw attention to them ("Can you find the same thing happening anywhere on the next page?"). Practise each appearance of it and see if there are any subtle variations such as a major third becoming a minor third halfway through.

At all times, draw attention to the printed music without actually expecting them to be able to "read" it unless they are fairly experienced. Say things like "Look at the second bar; do you see the long note? and how many short notes are there? Look at the word "peace" - how many notes are there on it? In the third line, which word do we go up on?" They'll be reading without effort before they know it.

In this way, by leaving it alone and simply expecting them as a matter of course to be able to extract small amounts of information from the music, sight-reading comes quickly and naturally. What does not work is the direct approach. "Right, now here's a new song. Let's see who can sight-read it!" will just invite a crisis of confidence.

Never use the old-fashioned books of "sight-reading exercises". They're a waste of time and paper.

Conducting

Most choirs sing best with a conductor, provided the conductor is good. If you have doubts about your own ability as a conductor, consider whether you actually need to conduct at all. If the choir know their work thoroughly, they can sing without a conductor. They will sing everything exactly as they learned it - tempo, dynamics etc. - and will be unable to introduce much flexibility, but they can do it. The biggest dangers are rushing and flatness, which you will be unable to correct as they occur. On the other hand, there is something attractive about a choir singing directly to the audience without the intervention of an adult.

However, assuming you <u>are</u> going to conduct, your main function is to remind the choir of the things they have learned in rehearsal - where the accents come, *crescendi* and *diminuendi*, particular words that require some emphasis or care etc. In comparison with orchestral conducting the "beat" is relatively unimportant, but be sure that the downbeat of each bar is in place and that the choir can recognise it.

Not watching the conductor is one of the few things you should bully your choir about. Almost everything else is more a matter of encouragement and praise, but personally I am quite unpleasant to sections of the choir who bury their heads in their copies and don't look up. If they persist, just walk up to them and gently take their music away. That usually does the trick!

Do practise in front of a mirror. Conduct every piece in your current repertoire, in full, with all repeats and at the correct speeds. Pay special attention to the joins between sections, and any changes of tempo. Follow the suggestions given below.

Conducting beginnings

The most important beat in any bar is not the down-beat at the beginning, but the up-beat before it. This is the beat on which the choir must breathe before making an entry (always make them breathe <u>together</u> and <u>in</u> <u>time</u> - the breath is part of the music). The up-beat tells them exactly where the down-beat is going to come, and describes the mood and style of the entry to come.

In front of your mirror, practise beginnings of many different kinds, making your up-beat exactly in tempo and reflecting accurately the style in which you wish them to make their entry - sharp and choppy for an energetic entry, large and expansive for a grand *forte* entry, smooth and caressing for a quiet entry and so on. The down-beat itself must have the same quality, expressing the music rather than just beating time. Try doing this with one hand - put the other in your pocket. With practice it should be possible to conduct an entire concert with only one hand. "Less is more"!

My suggestion to put one hand in your pocket is perfectly serious: never fall into the habit of conducting with both hands in mirror image of each other. It's not wrong, exactly, and it won't do the singing any harm, but it's terribly amateurish and any musicians in the audience will look down their noses at you - and don't pretend you don't care what people think; you do. And so you should – they're the <u>audience</u>, for goodness' sake!

Conducting the middle of the bar

Again, your beat must mirror the style in which the choir is to sing. A sharp, choppy beat will ruin a quiet, expressive piece, for instance. Do not become too absorbed in maintaining the traditional shape of the 3/4 or 4/4 beat, but concentrate on making the last beat and the first beat of each bar clearly. In between, concentrate on maintaining performance style and encouraging your singers.

Maintaining tempo while conducting

Young choirs can easily rush or drag. So can accompanists, for that matter. Sometimes this can be a good thing - it may be that their own feeling for the music is dictating a tempo that would be better than yours, so be alert to the possibility that they could be right and you wrong. One's own notion of tempo can sometimes be dictated not by the needs of the music but by the need to conduct comfortably and calmly. Many years ago I conducted a performance of Handel's *Messiah*, only to realise at the end that I had conducted every major chorus – *Hallelujah*, *All we like sheep*, *For unto us a child is born* etc. - at exactly the same speed. You wouldn't have thought this was possible, would you, but I'd managed it ...

If your choir does begin to rush, don't beat more furiously in an attempt to control them. They don't realise they are rushing, and will interpret your frenetic movements as encouragement to go even faster. Instead, make your movements broader, more smooth and flowing. Catch the eye of one or two stronger singers, and maintain eye-to-eye contact as you try to convey an impression of calmness. Smile at them, and don't give them the impression anything is wrong.

If they have begun to drag, once again establish eye contact with your leading singers. Try to convey encouragement, not agitation, and concentrate on the up- and down-beats of each bar, leaning forward slightly at each one as if you are saying "Look, here is the down-beat, wasn't that nice, and now come along, here comes the next one .... and here it is, well done, now let's prepare for the next ......" and so on. In the middle of the bar a sort of rolling movement almost as if you were winding a ball of wool is a good substitute for the normal beat-shape, and indicates forward movement rather well (many years ago I played in an orchestra conducted by a professor of conducting at a famous

London conservatoire. He conducted almost entirely in circles, and I don't remember him being particularly hard to follow. There's no point in being too precious about these things).

Conducting endings

Composers often judge the length of their last notes to a nicety, tying crotchets and quavers together to end precisely on the fourth quarter of the beat or whatever seems a good idea at the time. However, few choirs can manage this sort of thing with any precision, and it might not be realistic to expect a young choir to do so at all - there are more important things to worry about. I should feel no shame at all in changing endings so that as a rule the final sound comes neatly on the beat.

One of the worst choral conductors I know is terribly proud of his endings to words and phrases. Each final consonant is indicated with a tremendous chopping movement - and that, of course, is exactly what he gets; a final consonant that is accurately in place but dead, devoid of sense or meaning, and which spoils the sound that went before. Remember, <u>it is the ending of a word that controls the sound in the middle.</u>

When you indicate the end of a word or phrase, treat it just as you would the beginning. Prepare it, give a clear up-beat so the choir can see it coming, and make the actual movement fit the context. If the final sound is soft ("m" or "n" for instance, or a vowel) then stroke it off gently. If it is a consonant like "t" or "d", then a very small precise movement is needed, using your fingertips. Don't worry how small - the choir will see it fine, because of course you have trained them to be watching like hawks at this point. Don't "cut off" but try to feel that you're "closing off" instead. The final consonant that gives the most trouble is "s", which needs a lot of practice if it is not to sound like a basket of snakes. Tell your singers to make it as short and small as they can. If necessary, cheat by telling half the choir not to pronounce the "s" at all.

Any movement you make to indicate an ending should normally be upwards, with the palm of the hand turned up and not down. Endings of phrases are danger-points for flat singing as the breath begins to run out, so do everything you can to encourage your singers to support the sound to the last.

Practise your endings in the mirror - they are more important than beginnings. Any old choir can take a deep breath and begin together on a solid *mezzo-forte*. A really precise, well-judged ending performed with nuance and taste is a thing of great beauty and will send your audience away feeling that they have been listening to a choir of real quality.

Who are you looking at?

It's always tempting to bury your head in your copy while conducting, just as singers will do if you let them. Obviously this is unhelpful; if you expect them to know their music thoroughly, the least you can do is know it yourself. So ideally you will only be glancing down occasionally, so ... who are you going to look at?

There are occasions when your gaze can sweep across the whole choir, for instance at the beginning of a song when you need to, as it were, "gather them all up" and be sure that they are ready to start. But of course you can really only look at one person at a time, and if you make sure that person is the right one, it can become a useful tool.

In every section you will soon find that there are one or two singers who are stronger and know their music more thoroughly than the rest. They will probably be the ones who watch you most assiduously too, and be most effective at picking up your facial instructions. It is these leading singers who should be the focus of your attention. When an entry arrives, look to these singers; they'll be ready, and they'll come with you and bring the rest of their section with them. Once they're up and running, your attention can move on to the next section.

When something goes wrong - perhaps the pace is flagging, or the pitch; perhaps one section has come in on a wrong note, or missed an entry altogether (and that one's probably your fault for not bringing them in clearly) - it is these same leaders you should look to. They will be quickest to pick up on what you want. But don't forget that, however good they are, they are still children, and easily rattled or put off. Don't indicate impatience or anger to them, but keep your face and gestures encouraging.

Above all, think hard about what you want from them. Do you want them to pick up the pace? Lean into the first beat of each bar, and make the up-beat and the following down-beat very clear. Keep your face bright and lively. Are they rushing, so you want them to slow down? Make broad, smooth movements and show them a calm, serene face. Is the pitch slipping? Indicate the "lottery face" and make signs for "support". Have they missed an entry? Remember, show no annoyance - they'll know they've gone wrong, and will be worrying about how to get back in. Mouth the words at them and smile - they'll soon pick up.

They are your most valuable singers: treat them as friends. But don't forget they won't be there for ever. Try to identify younger singers who have the same virtues, and give them a bit of attention too. Next year it may be them you need to rely on.

Using your body when conducting

Use your body to say what you mean. Your conducting must only be as energetic as the music is. Don't jab and thrust in an effort to achieve more accuracy if the style doesn't suit those movements. Conventional wisdom says that one hand, usually the right, takes care of the beat while the other indicates expression, but I find I can do most of it with only one hand. Whichever hand you use, here are one or two tips ...

Don't lift your hand or hands too high, either to indicate *forte* or a high note. High hands will encourage them to make a similar movement with their heads, the chin will rise and the muscles of the throat become tense. Tone will become strained and the pitch will suffer. If they can see you well enough, it would be ideal to do most of your conducting no higher than your shoulders, to help them keep their chins down.

Nevertheless your choir will be watching your face as much as your hands, so use that too. To indicate *forte,* adopt a determined expression and more expansive beat. For *piano* singing, a palm turned downwards may make them sing softer but it is also negative and will encourage them to sing flat. It is better to use a facial expression - purse your lips as though saying "shhhh!".

The palm turned upwards is positive and encouraging and will have a beneficial effect on pitch. Do not use it too much though, and whatever you do don't raise it higher and higher as this will cause singers to strain.

However the downwards palm can be useful at times. For instance, when singing up a minor third, singers will instinctively make a nice flat interval if they see the palm turned down, but at the same time the whole hand can delineate in the air the upward movement of the music. For a major third, do the same but turn the palm upwards and raise your eyebrows.

Your singers will need constant reminders about where to breathe and where not to breathe. Even though they have practised this in rehearsal and marked their parts accordingly, they will still forget so you must remember for them. Indicate a breath by taking a breath yourself, lifting your head and your elbows slightly as you do so. To indicate those places where you have decided to "sing through" without a breath, make a long movement away from the body with one hand as though "carrying" the music through the phrase. These are important indications, and in a complex part-song you may have to make them to different sections of the choir at different times, so will need to know your score well.

Later in this book there is some advice on getting your choir to sing in tune. Your conducting must, of course, serve to remind them when it is necessary to put this advice into effect. Never suggest annoyance or worry - they are too busy singing to work out just what it is you are cross about. In the very rare event that they begin to sing sharp, simply make all your movements and facial expressions very relaxed and calming. Let your arms and shoulders flop a little to indicate a "dropping" of the voice, and turn your palms downwards. Darken your facial expression.

It is far more likely that they will go flat - all choirs do, from time to time. Here you need to indicate two main things - "support" and facial expression. My sign for support is a hand that travels smoothly up my chest from the navel, then turns smoothly outwards and "carries" the sound up and away from me into the air. For the facial expression I gesture to my face, drawing attention to my mouth which is open and smiling, and then to my eyes which also smile with raised eyebrows. As they have practised all these things in rehearsal, this is enough to remind them to put into effect all the "sharpening measures" we know. Without actually making them worry about it, I will have discussed flatness with them, presenting it as a fact of life that can be simply solved by the elementary techniques we have learnt - which of course it is, and can.

Singing yourself

If you can't or won't sing yourself, then you are going to be at a considerable disadvantage as a choir trainer. I suppose it can be done, but there are so many things that are hard to explain in words or demonstrate on the piano when you could just say "Listen, make it sound like *this*! ...."

Besides, children are great mimics. It is well-known that little boys joining church choirs for the first time just copy the sounds they hear around them. This has, over the years, created the almost unique and very beautiful English style of church music. You have probably heard little girls giving the most uncanny imitations of their favourite pop singers - often the same girls who can sound like little angels when they sing in your choir.

Personally I sing with my choirs a lot of the time in rehearsal, particularly when we are at the note-learning stage. But it's not a helpful habit, and over the years I have tried to stop myself doing it. For instance, there is a risk that you will hear what you are doing yourself, rather than paying attention to what they are doing. You may also hear what you want to hear - in other words, your imagination may supply accuracy that in reality is not there.

There is also a chance that you may start doing it in performance, which if like me you are a man conducting a girls' choir, will sound pretty strange! One is reminded of the great Canadian pianist Glenn Gould, who sang with himself while he played - not always in tune, to be honest.

Still, when teaching songs and at many other times, singing yourself is by far the best way to lead your choir. And there's one vital thing to bear in mind when you do it - pitching. If you are a man, remember that when you sing to your young choir they can easily misinterpret the pitch (octave) you are singing at. What they will be aware of, is whereabouts in your voice it feels to be. Sounds that are obviously high in your voice, they will reproduce high in their own. For instance, if you are a bass or baritone and you strain up to sing this .....

.... they will think you want them to sing .....

If you actually wanted ......

....you should have demonstrated at the same place in your own voice, thus ....

Marking parts

As all musicians know, it is normal and helpful to make pencil marks in printed music. You should encourage your choir to do so. Some people recommend a soft pencil, but in my experience this can be hard to erase and an HB pencil used lightly is best. But beware, idle hands in rehearsal will get carried away even with the best of intentions. Once after my choir had performed Brahms' *German Requiem* I found that one girl had written "Watch!!!" with three exclamation marks and four underlinings in big black letters at the top of every single page in the book, which was a bit self-defeating and murder to correct before taking the music back to the library.

Left to themselves, children tend to write in words exactly what you have said to them, so it's better to encourage them to use a few short-hand signs - for instance ....

 a smily face at places where the pitch tends to slip or the sound needs to be bright

 a frowny face at places where the sound needs to be dark or the pitch depressed (a useful sign for the alto section, in my experience)

 a curvy arrow up to indicate the need for support

 an arrow pointing forward for an *accelerando*

 an arrow pointing back for a *ritenuto*

 a wiggly line over the note for a *tenuto*

 a little pair of spectacles meaning "watch out, there's something nasty coming"

These signs are easily understood, and there's some value in using "standard" marking. After all, you might have to collect the music in for some reason, and next time they might not get their "own" markings back.

Summary

- *No single factor is half as important to the development of powerful, flexible and effective singing as a well-established warmup routine*

- *Pace your choir's work: there comes a point when they can't learn any more however hard they try*

- *When teaching new material, rely on their intelligence. They don't need to be spoon-fed <u>all</u> the time*

- *The most important part of a word or note is its ending, not its beginning*

- *Which particular singers are you conducting <u>to</u>?*

- *You can convey lots of information with your bodily movements; practise in front of a mirror*

- *When you sing yourself, think about pitch: what counts is not what note you sing, but where it is in your voice*

- *Encourage intelligent and discriminate marking of parts*

DEVELOPMENT - YOUR CHOIR IN TRAINING

Posture

At the beginning of each warm-up or rehearsal session, quickly run through the posture. And first, practise it yourself in front of a mirror. You can't teach it to your choir if you can't do it yourself.

The aim is to adopt a posture that they can maintain without effort for some time, that does not invite them to fidget, and that ensures that the surprisingly great weight of the head is borne by the vertical backbone to minimise muscular effort. *"Good posture is calm and quiet, flexible in all parts, and allows the body to give muscular support to the air-flow which propels and fuels the voice"* (Linda Hirst).

The feet should be a little apart, and one foot should be a little further forward than the other. In this way each singer has a firm base to stand on, with the weight evenly on both feet. Constantly correct them when they put all their weight on one leg, as they will be tempted to do. Otherwise, when that leg gets tired they will have to shift to the other, which creates fidgeting and distraction. The weight should be on the balls of the feet, not the heels, so that they feel lively and poised for action. Make them rise imperceptibly onto their toes every so often during rehearsal to remind them.

Many singing teachers and choir trainers say that the knees should not be locked back, but should remain slightly bent and flexible. I don't really see the point of this and think it could be distracting, so I don't bother about it.

The shoulders should be relaxed, not hunched up. Encourage them to imagine that their elbows are heavy and draw the shoulders downwards. Be sure that it is the ribs and not the shoulders that rise when breathing in.

The arms and hands should not flop down out of control but be relaxed and gently curved. Don't let them clasp their hands behind their backs, as this constrains the free expansion of the rib cage. Many professional singers place one hand on the stomach which feels right, but for a young choir it is probably better if the fingertips rest lightly on the front of the thighs - try it yourself and you will see that it enhances the "poised" feeling. Keep the elbows slightly away from the sides of the body.

The head should sit on top of the backbone. Make them imagine that a string is attached to the top of the head, drawing it gently upwards. They should "feel tall".

The <u>bottom</u> should be tucked in - make them clench their buttocks three or four times so they have to think about where their bottom is.

Naturally your choir will spend some time sitting down - it is not realistic to expect them to spend the whole of each rehearsal standing up or they will quickly become tired and fractious. When seated, encourage them to use only the front six inches of the chair, and not lean back into it while they sing. The same "feeling tall" idea applies, with the head drawn up as though by a string. A routine can help, so that for instance reading new music and basic note-learning are always done sitting down, but whenever you put it all together they stand up automatically. If you spend some time working with one particular section of the choir, encourage the other sections to sit down and wait without being told. Treat children as intelligent beings and that's exactly what they'll be.

When holding sheet music or books, whether sitting or standing make them use both hands and hold the music high so that its top is in line with the Adam's Apple (larynx). Then make them move it a little bit further away from them than feels quite normal, and cock the elbows outwards just a fraction, like oboists often do. In theory, this is to prevent the weight of the flesh of the upper arm bearing down on the ribs and inhibiting the breathing. In practice, it just looks good. Tell them that if they feel faintly unnatural and ridiculous, they're probably doing it right!

When two children are sharing a book, make each of them have one hand on it so that it is held centrally between them, and try to see that they are both about the same height. Some choir trainers make children share on purpose - it's much harder to bury their heads in the music if they're sharing with someone else.

The young voice and how it works

The young boy's voice is divided into two quite distinct parts, the head voice and the chest voice. The chest voice is the speaking voice, and in most boys will extend comfortably up to about B or C above middle C. The head voice comes in above that, and extends all the way up to the top - in some cases as high as C above the treble stave. Experienced boy singers are perfectly well aware of the two voices and can to some extent decide just when and where they will "change gear" and move from one to the other. Male choir-trainers understand the head voice very well, because it is exactly analogous to the adult male's *falsetto*, and besides they've been boys themselves.

The situation with girls is less well defined and harder to understand - especially for a man. I have asked many experienced female singers to explain to me just how a girl's voice feels, and they seem to find this difficult to do. The young girl's voice certainly has the same division between chest and head, but the difference is much less and many girls seem to be unaware of moving between them. There is also an area of comparative weakness between the two at about an octave above middle C, which I have heard some female singers liken to a third "middle" voice.

I have heard many singing teachers begin a lesson by singing scales upwards, getting a little higher each time. This is pointless and destructive. Working with both boys and girls - particularly with girls - your aim must be to bring the head voice down, and to discourage them from taking the chest voice up. Otherwise you'll get sounds of strain and ugly tone. You will notice that in our warm-up we definitely do not begin by singing upwards. When we eventually do start going up, it is in the octave exercise which enables them to swing widely over the break between their voices. The leaps are too great for them to be tempted to carry the chest voice upwards - they have to go straight into their heads (try it yourself and you'll see what I mean). With younger singers it is a good idea to actually teach them how to get into their head voices - some inexperienced children don't even realise they've got one. We talked about this in the section on singing in primary schools - remember Mrs.Butcher?

Managing the voice

Try this. Make your choir sing a little tune - something they know really well - while pretending to be thin, waif-like little creatures with pale faces and no confidence at all. Now make them sing the same tune while pretending to be great big, fat ladies with really wobbly voices. After a little amusement and embarrassment, they'll enjoy this. You could even play them a recording of different types of singers to show what you mean.

The purpose of this silliness is to show them - and yourself - that we all make the sound we want. By encouraging them to mimic, you can lead your young singers into discovering that they have far bigger, fuller voices than they ever dreamed. It just takes an effort of will.

You now have to turn this discovery into something useful, and to do so you must make sure that there is no undue effort or strain involved. For some long time you should outlaw loud singing, but instead encourage them to think in terms of "thin" singing and "fat" singing - it's a question of tone, not volume. Fat singing requires the chin to be dropped slightly: tell them to imagine they have a ping-pong ball inside their mouths, so that the inside of the mouth is nice and round.

This same principle of deciding what sort of sound you want to make and then making it, works extremely well with young tenors and basses. Some years ago I had a choir with a rather small number of tenors and basses aged 16 and upwards who really made a very weedy sound indeed. One day during a section rehearsal I made them imitate Luciano Pavarotti (or what they imagined Pavarotti sounded like) and they amazed themselves with the amount of sound they could produce - again, not loud but fat. They were so tickled with this discovery that they persuaded me to keep it a secret. The next day in full rehearsal they waited until they came to a section in which tenors and basses sung a unison melody together, and let rip. The effect was electric - the sopranos and altos nearly fell off their chairs! The choir never forgot this, and our tenor and bass sections never again had any difficulty balancing the girls.

All this notwithstanding, your choir should never be encouraged to force. You should NEVER nag a choir to sing louder - on the contrary, encourage them to sing softer most of the time. Power comes from the warm up - and it <u>will</u> come in time, I promise. When you do have a loud passage to sing, make them achieve the same effect by singing more clearly - by imagining that they are forming the words right out in front of their faces, shooting their lips forward - but not, not, NOT shouting.

There is one very effective technique, however, that <u>does</u> involve some effort. You frequently find places in a piece of music where there is a leap upwards to a high note to make a climax. In such places you can achieve an excellent effect by making the choir do all the work on the lower note or notes before the leap - in effect, a hefty *crescendo*. Then as they go for the high note, back off completely, as though it were marked *subito piano*. In this way they can achieve effortless high notes and a very good effect of climax without any strain, mainly by distracting their attention from the high note itself because they're so busy thinking about its preparation. The high notes are thus "placed" naturally and without tension, and the tone will improve overall.

Tone

I repeat, tone and volume - in fact almost "all things bright and beautiful" - come from a carefully planned set of warm-up exercises. If your warm-up is being effective, in the rest of your rehearsal you can concentrate on learning notes and working out interpretation without having to worry about where the sound is coming from - it'll be there, very soon. In the course of normal singing however ....

- Good tone comes from .... the words. We need to secure lively, mobile faces with a good variety of mouth-shapes. Encourage your singers to make as many faces as they can while they sing - it's the only chance they'll ever have to make faces at a teacher and get away with it! A good piece of homework is to sit in front of a mirror and read, or talk, or recite poetry to themselves. Many will be surprised how static their faces are normally. Tell them to try and look as though they have rubber faces instead.

- Good tone comes from .... the eyes. I have no time for those ignorant people who feel that a choir must look as though it's deliriously happy all the time. Singing is a serious business, and the time for a big grin is when the audience claps. Don't make your choir smile while singing <u>except</u> (a) on those vowels that require it e.g. "nice", "peace" etc. where it is definitely necessary to make the right sound, or (b) when it is necessary to control the pitch. BUT the eyes <u>can</u> smile most of the time. We have talked elsewhere about the "lottery face" - the expression of delighted surprise that draws the cheekbones up and shapes the face.

- Good tone comes from .... a free and continuous flow of air both in and out. The aim is to take plenty of air in, and then use it up again without letting the lungs collapse completely. If they have to gasp or pant, or hold on desperately until the end of a long note, they (or you) have done something wrong. On the other hand there are no brownie points for ending up with ten gallons of spare air in their lungs. They must breathe when they need to, in musically appropriate places, taking in as much as they need and no more. Then they must use it. See the section below about "Breathing".

- Good tone comes from .... the careful control of word/note endings. The endings are more important than the beginnings (frankly, beginnings are easy). The endings inform and control what goes before. Keep the sound going and support it carefully with breath and posture until it is time to put the final consonant on. Even then don't relax - they mustn't "sag" until the sound is properly finished. If the word ends with sounds like "n" and "m", sing right through those sounds in a lengthy hum, always well supported. In the middle of phrases, put the final consonant of a word onto the beginning of the next word, not only to keep it together but so that the preceding vowel stays open until the last moment.

| Roun | dan | droun | dwe | wen | tall | day |
| (Round | and | round | we | went | all | day) |

- Good tone comes from .... a free and continuous flow of <u>sound</u>, too. It is a great mistake to allow the pursuit of excellent diction to break the music up too much. Exaggerated beginnings of words and sharp, percussive ends may make the words clear, but can be destructive. Practise singing with just the vowel shapes but no consonants, to get the feeling of an unbroken flow of sound and tone.
- Good tone comes from .... constant attention to the "placing" of the voice, especially where the music moves frequently from high to low and back. As in the "semitone" warm-up exercise, remind your singers to imagine the "source" of the voice moving as appropriate, from head to chest etc.
- And good tone comes from .... constant attention to the type of sound they want to make. Remind them frequently about "thin sound and fat sound", or Luciano Pavarotti or what have you. But always explain very clearly what you want - singing "fat" is not the same as singing loudly. All too often children's response to any kind of encouragement is to sing louder, which is not the point at all.

Focus

Once you are satisfied that your choir are producing an easy, open tone with plenty of breath to carry it, you can produce a further improvement by "focusing" the sound. Too many choirs have been taught to sing with their mouths gaping wide, which spoils the tone completely.

Encourage them to keep the <u>insides</u> of their mouths nice and big - remember imagining they have a ping-pong ball in there - but to sing through a comparatively small opening. Let them stick just one finger between their teeth - for most vowel sounds, that's wide enough. An analogy some may appreciate is the difference between a blunderbuss and a rifle. The blunderbuss was an old type of gun with a very wide barrel. You loaded it with shot, old nails, pebbles etc. and some gunpowder, fired it off and anything in a twenty yard radius got peppered willy-nilly. A rifle on the other hand has a narrow bore and fires one single bullet exactly where you point it. You want your singers to be rifles, not blunderbusses.

Singing in parts

Children mostly want to sing the tune. Don't let them. We have already discussed the question of balance and the need to make sure that the top part - usually the melody - is not the strongest. However many you have on each part, you need to adopt certain strategies to counter the tyranny of the melody, and to teach your singers to be comfortable on harmony lines. Inexperienced singers in the lower sections will tend to wander off onto the tune if you let them, so try to sit them among stronger, more experienced singers.

When beginning a new song, tackle the middle and bottom parts first. It's not a bad idea to make the whole choir try, say, the second soprano part, and then the alto part before they've even heard the melody. This will destroy any mystique about part-singing and help them realise that all parts are equally difficult. Even after the parts have been learnt, expect everybody to sing all the parts at least occasionally - "now, the seconds need to practise this bit, so let's sing it with them - it'll be good practice for us all." And in some pieces make the first and second sopranos swap parts permanently. The seconds will like it, and the firsts will understand that it's only fair.

Your first soprano section will make the fewest mistakes. Your second sopranos will make more, but provided there are a lot of them - substantially more than in the firsts - they should be strong enough to fend for themselves. Your alto section will need a certain amount of Tender Loving Care, however. They are young, remember, and not very experienced at singing a low part. There probably won't be many of them, either. And, most important, they are having to listen to the bottom of the harmony all the time. This is hard for young people who have always been used to paying attention to the melody, unless you are lucky enough to have among them children who play bass instruments like the cello, double-bass or bassoon. Also, much of their part lies at the lower extremity of their voices and they may therefore experience difficulty in hearing whether they are in tune or not, or even on the right note at all.

Encourage the altos to listen actively by cupping their hands behind their ears like folk-singers sometimes do, or pressing two fingers on their temples (I'm not sure this actually helps them hear themselves any better, but they'll think it does, which is the main thing). Make the sopranos sing very softly while the altos practise their own part, so they can hear themselves without too much distraction. Allow the altos to sing a little more strongly than the other sections. And try to get them into the habit of thinking graphically about the music they are singing: Kodaly-type signs would be useful but failing that let them trace the shape of the music in the air with one hand so that each leap up or down is linked to a distinct physical movement. And finally, give your altos a lot of encouragement. Tell them you know they have a difficult job, and make sure the rest of the choir know it too. Praise their sound and encourage them to use their rich chest-tones. Don't let them try too hard on the very lowest notes or they'll go sharp. And don't criticise them when they go adrift. Altos are allowed to make mistakes.

One last tip about part-singing. Protect your first sopranos from too much effort which will create strain and ugly tone. They are going to be heard anyway, just because they are on top. At climaxes especially if their part is quite high, make sure they sing comfortably within themselves and rely on the high pitch to give them carrying-power. Meanwhile, encourage the lower parts to give them lots of support. Because their notes are lower they can "give it some welly" without sounding strained and raucous. It is the second sopranos who are the power-house of the choir, and it is they and the altos who must do most of the work in creating the climax, so that the firsts can just ride beautifully on top of the body of sound.

Singing from memory

It's always better to sing from memory if you can manage it. It looks good and sounds good, and your singers will have no difficulty watching the conductor so you will find them more flexible and responsive.

Don't make a big deal of learning music from memory. In fact, don't attempt to <u>learn</u> from memory at all - just wait until you think they are ready, make them put the copies away, and spring it on them with the assurance that if they forget the words it's OK to "la, la, la". Mouth the words at them to help their memories - usually just the first word or two of each phrase is enough. BUT don't tell them off if they can't do it. They are allowed to make mistakes, and can always do it better next week - and if it's the actual concert next week, you planned it badly, didn't you?

Articulation

I used to worry about the words a lot and spent much rehearsal time on them, and my audiences frequently complimented us on the clarity of our diction. Then I stopped bothering nearly so much about the words and - guess what? They still complimented us on the clarity of our diction! I am, though, very careful about my own diction when singing or speaking to them - vowel sounds, rolled Rs etc. - and they do tend to copy what they hear.

All too often children's response to being told to sing the words more clearly is simply to sing them more loudly. Practise diction softly to avoid this, but do NOT make them speak or whisper the words, only sing them. Whispering in particular is very tiring to the voice and does little good. Instead, encourage your singers to (a) "make the faces" - sing with as much variety of face and mouth shape as they can, and (b) imagine that they can bring the words right out in front of their faces, so that lips and tongues and teeth feel as though they are working away in mid-air.

The beginnings of words are the easiest to deal with, and for this reason many choir-trainers over-emphasise them. In fact the endings are much more important as they inform and shape the vowel sound and therefore the tone that fills the middle of the note. Make your choir "sing through" every ending, supporting the tone with the breath all the way, cutting nothing short and allowing nothing to sag. Talk about "looking after" the endings. Many words contain several sounds, and both tone and diction will improve if you encourage your choir to "love" each sound as it passes. For instance, the word "hands" contains an aspirated "h", an open "a" sound, a resonant, humming "nnn", a thick, heavy plosive "d" and the final "sss" which can sometimes be modified to "zzz" if another vowel comes next. All these sounds are important, and each needs to be cared for.

When singing I always roll my "r" if it comes at the beginning of a word, and encourage my choirs to do the same. Not all of them can manage it, and I have not yet discovered a way of teaching them. It may be that a quirk of physiology makes it impossible for some people to do. Nevertheless I soldier on, and suggest you do too.

Naturally entries that begin with a plosive sound like "k" or "t" will have the consonant exactly on the beat. On the other hand, where the consonant is not plosive - for instance, "m" or rolled "r" - it is the following <u>vowel</u> that comes on the beat. Make your choir think of the music actually beginning as the mouth springs open for the vowel.

Make your diction suit the circumstances, and don't be afraid to "cheat" if it will improve the sound. For instance, in Saint-Saens' *Ave Maria* the lower part has an entry on *"Sancta Maria, mater Dei ..."* which, being low and needing resonance, sounds much better if you sing "Zzar - nng - da Mar - rrri - ar", thus keeping the sound back in the resonating part of the head instead of pushing it to the front of the mouth where there is little resonance.

There are also occasions where the opposite approach works well. Particularly sensitive sounds are the vocalised plosive consonants like "d", "b" and "g". These are made with the lips, tongues and teeth like all consonants, but have the weight of the voice behind them. Try singing "digger, digger, digger" and then "ticker, ticker, ticker" slowly to yourself and you will feel what I mean. The action of lips, tongue and teeth are pretty much identical, but on the vocalised plosives in "digger" the larynx itself is working.

When children are singing fairly high up, or very softly, the introduction of these vocalised plosives can disrupt the stream of tone. Not only does the sound momentarily stop, but for a split second the larynx feels as though it is producing a much lower sound than the high tessitura of the phrase. On the other hand, if you replace "d" with "t" the effect on the tone-stream is much less, and in most cases the audience won't know the difference. For instance, at the beginning of John Gardner's *Waly, waly* we sing "Town in the meadows the other day" instead of "Down in the meadows ....". This makes it easier to gently pitch this very soft and subtle entry ...

Similarly at the second phrase of Saint-Saens' *Ave Maria*, replacing "g" with "k" and thus singing "kratia plena" will help the first sopranos to float onto their top F sharp without the encumbrance of that weighty throat-closing "g" sound.

In other places and other pieces, "p" can often take the place of "b" to similar effect.

A difficult consonant is "h". It is hard to make this audible sometimes, and it wastes air. If you have an "h" sound in a particularly important place, try raising the tongue at the back of the mouth and producing a slightly guttural sound like the "ch" in German, as in "Ich bin". Used with restraint this can take the place of "h", is easier to hear and uses much less air.

This cavalier tinkering with the words will probably offend purists and trained singers. What we have to bear in mind is that we are not dealing with trained singers, but with children who are available to us for only limited amounts of rehearsal and voice tuition. In our circumstances, any short-cut that produces the right effect and does no damage must be justified.

An interesting thought: Madeleine Marshall's authoritative book *The Singer's Manual of English Diction* has no less than twenty-two chapters on consonants. Wow!

English has more different vowel sounds than most languages, which must make it very difficult for foreigners to learn. Italian, for instance, has only five vowels - "a" (pronounced as a broad "ah"), "e" (pronounced rather like "air"), "i" (pronounced "ee"), "o" (pronounced rather like "or") and "u" (pronounced like "should"). English on the other hand has thirteen vowel sounds and the differences between them are very subtle. Jean Ashworth Bartle quotes a sentence from Dorothy Park: "Through good known thoughts of art, love learns and then takes his ease". Say this slowly to yourself several times and you'll get the point. An additional difficulty is that many vowels in English are actually diphthongs - in other words, two vowels run together. The most common are ...

"ah-ee" as in "smile" or "child" "ah-oo" as in "now" or "round"
"oh-ee" as in "boy" or "voice" "ay-ee" as in "gay" or "sail"
"oh-oo" as in "float" or "goal"

With all of these your choir should be encouraged to move to the second part of the diphthong as late as they can, right at the end of the vowel. For instance, "child" sounds best as "chaaaaaaaaa-ild". The exception is "ee-oo" as in "youth" or "beauty", where it is best to move off the "ee" and onto the "oo" as soon as possible.

I dare say it is possible to make lots of rules about how the thirteen vowel sounds and the diphthongs should be sung. Probably someone already has. My own method is to spend a lot of time singing or mouthing the words of each song to myself, asking myself "just what sound is that supposed to be, what do I want it to sound like, and how am I doing it?" I then make my choirs do the same.

Simple really.

Breathing

Breathing is, of course, the life-blood of everything your choir does. The initial exercise in your warm-up routine should help your singers to respect and think about their breathing. Apart from that I do no specific breathing exercises, but I do devote a considerable amount of rehearsal time to it. If singers' breathing and their use of the breath is imperfect, tone and pitch will suffer immediately. So ....

- Getting the breath in (1): Frequently remind them to maintain upright posture, keep the shoulders relaxed, and feel the ribs rise with the inward breath. Discourage them from breathing too deeply - they don't need a complete lungful so they feel stuffed, but a comfortable three-quarters or seven-eighths.

- Getting the breath in (2): where there is time to do so, insist that your choir breathe in rhythm and together, so that the inwards breath is as much part of the music as the actual sound. For instance:

- Getting the breath in (3): encourage them to "feel" each other breathing - look out of the corners of their eyes, let their heads and elbows lift slightly as they breathe and be aware of the rest of the choir doing the same. Breathe with them yourself while conducting. The choir that breathes together, sings together!

- Getting the breath in (4): in between phrases there is often little time to take a breath. It will take a lot of practice and nagging, but you can persuade them to <u>make</u> the time for a breath. At the end of the phrase, support the sound to the end and "look after" the last note, not cutting it short or allowing it to sag. Then take the breath; then without any sense of urgency begin the next phrase. If this means that the music will lift off the tempo for a moment and the accompanist has to be flexible, that's fine. That's what we have good accompanists for. Practise and practise this over and over to get it together. There is always time to take a breath however quick the music. It is they who are in charge of the music, not the music in charge of them!

- Getting the breath in (5): your choir need to breathe frequently, and you should avoid making them go too long without a breath. However, there are some places that are very bad to breathe in. These are usually the places where everyone <u>wants</u> to breathe, and because of this they are very obvious to the listener. Sing this for example .....

All right, so you will naturally take a breath after "sun" - that's self-evident. But then don't you feel yourself dying to take a breath towards the end of the first crotchet of "day", before getting into the semiquavers? Of course you do! Or if not there, then certainly at the end of the next crotchet, or the one after that. And in the second phrase you probably want to do the same after the first note of "lark". However, these places are so obvious that you absolutely must not breathe there. In fact the second phrase really needs to be sung entirely in one breath. In general, then, to give your audience the impression of a single, seamless flow of sound, seek out all the places where your singers will naturally tend to breathe, and <u>don't let 'em!</u>

- Getting the breath in (6): well, you may be saying, that's all very well but how do I avoid having half my choir turn blue and fall off the stage? The answer lies in the old idea of "secret breathing". While singing a long melismatic run or holding a long note, you breathe and then join in again, but you make sure that you don't do it at the same time as the person next to you - and the audience is none the wiser.

With children you can take this a step further. They love the mischief of it, and you can make it a wonderful game - "look, I want to hear this long phrase sung entirely in one breath. You <u>can</u> breathe, of course, but you'd better not let me hear you or see you! Now then, I'm going to be watching like a hawk ...... 1,2 ......" You will find that with practice they become very good at this. Strangely, when you do catch them out it is usually because you have heard the breath, not seen it being taken.

● Getting the breath in (7): your choir's pitching and intonation will be greatly improved if you teach them to breathe "at pitch". For instance, look at the beginning of one of my favourite pieces, Saint-Saens' *Ave Maria*, already quoted above ....

This opening is difficult to bring off. Assuming that they're going to breathe in together on the fourth beat, they only have three beats to listen to the piano and think about finding their own notes. Consequently, they often grope for the first note.

The answer is (a) to prepare the notes by internalising (imagining) them throughout the three beats, (b) to prepare their bodies by standing in exactly the same posture they will use when they begin singing, and most importantly (c) to breathe in on the fourth beat "at pitch". I'm not saying that they can <u>actually</u> breathe in and make a top E or C sharp, but they can <u>pretend</u> to. And having done so, you will find they make the entry cleanly and with considerable accuracy, because psychologically it is no longer the first note - their brains have already sung it!

Now, having got the breath in, how do we use it?

- Using the breath up (1): your singers should aim never to feel less than half full of air. If they approach the end of a phrase with less than that in their lungs, even if they manage to last out, the tone will fade and the pitch sag towards the end. They will develop the knack of metering the air out so it lasts longer, but when all is said and done they do have to breathe and <u>should</u> breathe when they need to. But they mustn't let it show!

- Using the breath up (2): SUPPORT! I am not sure whether this is something you do <u>with</u> the breath or something you do <u>to</u> it. I just know it is essential, but explaining it to your young singers is not very easy. Michael Brewer (National Youth Choir of Great Britain) talks of cradling a large furry animal in your arms. I presume he means an imaginary one, or choir-practices could be ... quite interesting. It's a nice image, though, useful when singing scales or scalic passages.

  My own image is a little different. Tell your choir to imagine they can pick the sound up with the upturned palm of one hand somewhere in the region of their belly-buttons, and lift it slowly and smoothly up their chests. On reaching the breast-bone, the hand begins to carry the sound away from the body and eventually "wafts" it gently into the air as though it were a balloon or soap bubble. Even after it has left the hand the support is not finished, for with an outstretched palm they can wave the sound goodbye as it floats lightly up and away into the distance.

  Now let them quietly sing a long, fairly high note and make the same motions, picking the sound up and carrying it gently away from them, following it as it floats away into the air. They will giggle and feel embarrassed, I expect, but you must insist. Frequently refer to this during rehearsal, and make the whole pantomime part of your own conducting technique. Use it when they sing up or down a scalic passage, or towards the end of a particularly long phrase, or when they are holding a long note. And in rehearsal at the appropriate places, insist that they actually go through the motions while they sing, in order to imprint the idea in their minds.

- Using the breath up (3): One of the things that will most impress your audience is the choir's ability NOT to take breath at obvious places. However, you do have to make it <u>plain</u> to the audience that this is happening, or what's the point? The way to do this is with a *crescendo*, for instance ....

Apart from the musical and "publicity" value of such a dynamic, there is the technical advantage that your singers will find it hard to take a breath while they are making the *crescendo*.

They will, of course, have been employing their "secret breathing", or the whole phrase will be too long for them.

The effect of this trick is very telling and professional, but do not overdo it - the total amount of *crescendo* should not be very great.

73

- Using the breath up (4): Do try to choose at least one song each term with a very long last note - it's excellent practice for them at "metering out" and controlling their breath, and gives a good opportunity to practise what you have taught them about supporting the sound. If you come across one of these songs that has a very long held note at the end, with a long *diminuendo* or *morendo* (dying) or *a niente* (to nothing) marking, and the choir find this difficult even with all the tricks you have taught them, consider cheating. Towards the end of the note, once it has become very soft indeed, they can move onto a "siren" (a "nggg" sound as used in the warmup) which will use practically no breath and can be sustained far longer and softer than an open note. If there is a consonant on the end, no problem - just put it on quietly and neatly. Let them move onto the siren at different times, and make them maintain the same vowel/mouth shape throughout or the audience will spot the deception.

Singing in tune

Your choir won't be able to sing in tune if they can't hear themselves - by which I mean that each individual singer needs to be able to hear his or her own voice as well as those around them. In some acoustics this may mean not standing too close together.

I encourage my choirs to do something physical about this: they either cup their hand behind one ear like folk-singers sometimes do, or press two fingers on their temple about midway between eyebrow and ear. Just how effective these two methods really are, I am not sure. The main thing is that the children think they are able to hear themselves better, possibly because it serves to concentrate their attention and makes them think about their intonation more. One hand behind the ear and the other cupped six inches in front of the mouth really does work ..... but it looks so stupid!

If you have a child or children who find particular difficulty in singing at the same pitch as everyone else, I suggest you ....

(a) stand them in the centre of a group of strong singers for a couple of weeks so they get a good, ingrained idea of the sound they are supposed to be making, and then ....

(b) move them to the edge or back of the section for a week or so to give them the opportunity to hear themselves better.

(c) Do not tell them they are at fault - I do sometimes go so far as to say "Oh, second sopranos, I thought someone was having a little wander just then! Cup your hands and have a good listen this time, won't you?" Persevere and ignore them. In my experience they often improve quite quickly. I believe the warm-up exercises help a lot as they get into the habit of manipulating and moving around in their voices.

(d) Of course, I am talking about mild cases, fortunately the majority. Very occasionally you may come across a child who is a real "groaner". Although even these will definitely improve with time and practice, you may have to decide that for the good of the whole ensemble they should be treated kindly but firmly: "I don't think you are quite ready for the choir just yet, so I'd like you to wait another year ...." and hope they forget about it in the meantime! This is harsh, but fortunately there are other musical avenues open to them. It's just that your choir doesn't have to be one of them.

We have already mentioned breathing "at pitch" - imagining that you can actually breathe on the note you are about to sing. Let's take that a little further: when a breath or short rest appears in the middle of a high passage like this .....

Here there is a great danger that having sung the top F natural, the first sopranos will relax while they breathe and then fail to quite crank themselves up again for the top F at the beginning of the next phrase.

The answer is not to allow their bodies or brains to come down from the height they have attained. Make them maintain their posture, and breathe "at pitch" on the top F. Thus their imaginations and bodies will not lose the "feeling" of the top F, and they will hit it again without difficulty. Tell them to think of moving "across" rather than "down and up again".

Physical attitudes that will help maintain pitch are a lively face with a variety of mouth-shapes, and smiling eyes with raised eyebrows - the "lottery face".

While conducting, gesture to the corners of your mouth and eyes if you feel the pitch slipping, and smile yourself. When hitting high notes, they should drop the chin very slightly to keep the muscles of the throat relaxed. When singing downwards passages - always a dangerous time as they tend to relax too much and each interval becomes a little too large - make them think "support" and rise ever so slightly on their toes. The first soprano part in the last two bars of the previous musical example is a case in point.

Whenever the music "rests" for a moment, by remaining on a long held note or some repeated pattern of notes of approximately the same pitch, renew your signals for "support", inviting them while they have time to think about it to carry the sound up and away into the building.

"Internalising" entries works really well. If they sing an entry out of tune, make them close their eyes and silently imagine that they are singing it. Then quickly make them open their eyes and do it for real. It will be far more in tune the second time.

An old church choirmaster's trick is to make the choir sing one note while "imagining" another. This takes considerable concentration and aural perception, but if they can do it there will certainly be an improvement in intonation. Wait until they are holding a longish note, then ask them to think about the note a semitone above it.

When the upper part goes particularly high, you can make their life much easier by encouraging the lower part(s) to give them a real "boost". A very good example is the wonderful climax of Fauré's gorgeous *Ave Maria* .....

.... where the seconds, by working hard on a pronounced *crescendo* on the low E sharp can spring themselves up to a strong top E sharp, and provide a solid base of sound which buoys the firsts up beautifully as they soar to the top B. It does look horrendous, but mine have never missed it.

Young altos - and young basses to a lesser extent - have a particular problem with pitching when very low down. They can't hear themselves very well, and will sometimes be markedly sharp. This is worse in fast pieces - in slow music they do have time to listen to their own voices and those of the rest of the choir, and make (usually unconscious) adjustments. Encourage them to use the physical means of listening to themselves - the cupped hand or the fingers on the temple - and identify and mark their music at the dangerous places. A "frowny" face and a feeling of "sitting down on the music" will help - see the section below on "How to sing flatter".

How to sing sharper

There are phrases in some songs that always seem to be flat whatever you do. There is one high passage for the 1st sopranos in Saint-Saens' *Ave Maria* that we can never get completely in tune, and there seems to be no reason for it. A pity, because otherwise it is not too difficult a piece provided the choir can "internalise" and hit their first notes accurately, and it sounds really classy! On the other hand, in Richard Rodney Bennett's *The Widow Bird* (one of his very fine unison cycle *The Aviary*) there is a passage where the opening tune is repeated very high and quite softly, yet I have never had a choir sing this other than perfectly in tune with no effort at all. Presumably it must be something about the actual construction of the music, the disposition of the leaps and steps and the placing of the words. It must be very skilfully written, but I can't for the life of me work out how!

Most choirs sing flat at some time. Obviously, the most dangerous times are at the beginning of a session before they've got into the swing of things, and towards the end of the session when muscles and concentration are flagging. Unaccompanied singing is most vulnerable. If you are rehearsing unaccompanied and you become aware that the pitch is slipping, don't make a big thing of it and continually correct them - sometimes it's better to ignore it and press on (although on the other hand it will eventually affect the altos' ability to reach their low notes).

The reasons for flat singing are usually (a) lack of confidence, (b) poor breathing, (c) strained voice production, (d) not listening or not internalising, (e) tiredness, (f) falling phrases, especially falling chromatic phrases, and/or (g) poor support of the voice.

Some solutions to these problems are .....

(a) Lack of confidence. Be sure that you have matched the material to the ability of the singers, and ensure that the material is very well known before you begin to make a big issue of the pitching. The first read-through of a new song is <u>not</u> a good time to complain about poor intonation!

(b) Poor breathing. Encourage your choir to breathe frequently, never letting the lungs be more than half empty. Discourage them from taking great gulps of air, but train them to take little sips when they have the chance, and to look for opportunities to practise intelligent secret breathing. They often run short of breath at phrase ends, which consequently "droop" in an unattractive way. Don't let them clip the ends of phrases short, but insist that they "look after" the last note and sing it right to the end, supporting all the time and taking care of every sound. For instance, if the last word is "sound", make them keep a long round vowel, and then resonate the "n" thoroughly before putting on the last consonant. Speak of "loving" the last note, or even stroking it as though it were a cat.

(c) Not listening or not internalising. Encourage singers to listen to the piano and to each other. If they are singing in parts, make them all sing each part in turn (good sight-reading practice). Then sing the passage with one part loud and the others very soft, taking it in turns. Teach them to exercise control over what their ears are doing by singing their own part and listening only to themselves; then singing it again but trying at the same time to listen to one of the other parts, or to the piano. Where they have a rest before an entry, teach them to "internalise" the note first by silently imagining they are singing it before actually doing so - this works very well.

Sometimes flat singing occurs because a certain note is simply too short. If singers don't have time to "settle" onto a note before moving to the next one, they can't listen to themselves and correct the pitch if necessary. If you suspect this to be the case, make them sing the phrase, stop on the offending note and hold it, and listen carefully to themselves. Usually this is all it takes to allow them to memorise (internalise) how the note feels and sounds. *Staccato* passages are difficult in this respect, and are also dangerous because they disrupt the smooth flow of breath.

(d) Strained voice production. While maintaining good upright posture, remind them to drop their chins slightly on the higher notes to avoid tightening up, especially when leaping upwards. Bending the knees very slightly also helps.

(e) Tiredness. Pace your rehearsals, changing the activity frequently to avoid boredom. They'll feel less tired singing quick songs, so keep these back for the end of a session. Think carefully about the length of each session. Young people can surprise you by their ability to keep going during long rehearsals, especially if they enjoy the way you work, but there are limits .....

(f) Falling phrases, especially falling chromatic phrases. These go flat quickly and frequently. Practise singing semitones, saying "this is the smallest interval you can possibly sing - I bet you!" Pick out little phrases and sing them slowly while thinking very carefully about the succession of tones and semitones therein. In performance, make "tiny, tiny" signs at them with your thumb and forefinger together; they'll remember what you mean. Make them think about supporting the sound while descending. Make them think of Michael Brewer's heavy, furry animal cradled in their arms while singing, lifting it a little higher with each descending interval.

(g) Poor support. Again, think about Michael Brewer's furry animal. Alternatively, do what I suggested earlier - make them imagine they are picking up the sound with one hand, gently carrying it away from their mouths and then wafting it out into the room as though it were an almost weightless balloon or a bubble. Insist that they actually mime the action with you. This works well in maintaining pitch during long held notes. I frequently make this motion to the choir while I am conducting.

Never criticise your choir for singing flat. It is important that they realise this is a common and natural occurrence, that all choirs do it, and that they need to listen for it, learn to detect it and master these techniques for avoiding it or putting it right. You should, however, tell them off for being too lazy or forgetful to use the techniques once they have learnt them. And remember, **the best and most effective single method of avoiding flat singing is the "lottery face" - that expression of delighted surprise that raises the eyebrows and cheekbones, opens the eyes and makes the whole face smile**. We actually draw little "smily faces" into our music if we find places that habitually go flat.

How to sing flat

It seems silly to include a section on deliberately singing flat, but occasionally you do find youngsters who sing sharp because they are trying too hard. They must be instructed to relax and sing softly. You can spot them because they breathe with their shoulders or sing with their chins up and a tight throat.

In the famous "Blues Brothers" film, the singer who takes the very lowest parts in the ensemble numbers has a nice dark brown voice, but he isn't a real *basso profundo* and just can't get down to some of his notes, so is sometimes as much as a semitone sharp. The same thing can happen to young altos or basses singing at the very bottom of their range.

The trick is exaggerated relaxation - if they worry or try too hard, they'll stay sharp. Practise actually flopping down into a chair on the lowest note. Then stay standing but "think sitting" - the voice just drops as it were under its own weight. Describe it as "sitting down" on a note. Talk of of "smily notes" and "frowny notes". While conducting, a down-turned palm encourages flatness, although it's a very negative and discouraging sign so not to be used much.

Singing unaccompanied

Children's ability to pitch notes is just as good as most adults. Practise it, and expect good pitching as a matter of course. Just take it for granted that having finished one song on a chord of G, they can work out the next one that starts in C. By all means show them how .... "Second sopranos, you finished on a G and your new note is E, three below. Let's hear you do that .... 1, 2, 3 and that's your note, yes! Now, firsts, you had a D and you need the C below it so your job is easy; let's hear that? ... " and so on, but if you don't make a fuss about it, nor will they.

Also, if you have stopped during a rehearsal to make some point, expect them to start again on the right notes without any help from the piano. Sometimes they'll be right and sometimes they won't, but they'll learn very fast. Once again, let them think this is normal, and it will become so. During the warm-up I frequently say "Right, that exercise was in G major. Sing me a B flat for the next one, please?" or "Good, now sing that again a tone and a half higher ..." or what have you.

Once they have got the hang of this, you can pull some very fancy stunts in performance - for instance, end one piece, then while the audience are clapping, quietly hum and work out the notes for the next one, and start without the intervention of the piano - very impressive. Or, if your first piece is unaccompanied, why not give them their notes in the changing room and let them carry the chord in their heads onto the stage. The audience will wonder how you did it.

In practical terms there is not, so far as I have learned, a great difference between singing with the piano or singing *a cappella* apart from the obvious one that, since they will not have the support of the piano, they will need to be even more secure in their learning than usual. Intonation may suffer, though, and this can have the unfortunate effect that we have mentioned earlier, namely that your young altos are already grovelling around at the very bottom of their voices, and if the pitch slips during the course of a piece they may find they can no longer reach the lowest notes at all. I have known this throw an alto section so completely that the whole second half of the piece was ruined.

If this happens to you repeatedly in rehearsal and you know that your choir are already earnestly using all the pitch-maintaining techniques you have taught them, then frankly I would advise taking the easy way out. Let them sing with a light piano accompaniment. There is little to be gained from the macho approach - your musical quality and the children's confidence could be badly damaged, and the audience are not likely to care (or even know) one way or the other.

Solos

It is terribly tempting to give any solos that come along to the same people all the time - you probably have two or three singers you know are reliable, and sound good, and don't get too nervous. But you need to think of the future, when those singers are no longer around. You also have a duty to other members who might like the chance. A good safety measure is to double up on all solos - by trial and error you can probably find two voices that will blend so well the audience won't know how many people are singing. Your soloists will feel more confident, and you have a backup in case one of them is ill. If you have more than one concert, they can take turns.

Communication

In choral competitions one word the adjudicators frequently use is "communication", yet sadly this is one thing we choir-trainers often forget because we are concentrating so hard on producing the best sound we possibly can.

By "communication" we mostly mean facial and body movement. Lively faces that make the most of the different word/mouth shapes are interesting and attractive. Eyes that sparkle and smile (the "lottery face") endear themselves to the audience, enliven the sound and maintain the pitch. Audiences and adjudicators are always impressed by singers who watch the conductor like hawks because this shows concentration and rapport. I am often told "Their eyes never left your face!" (poor little things, that can't be much fun).

Few young singers will do all this naturally but it can be taught. Some of it will arise anyway from your training in diction and pitch control, while you are probably already making your choir move when breathing together before an entry, or when "nodding themselves off" at the end of a phrase. Your singers certainly will watch you like hawks if your face and gestures give them a constant stream of cues and reminders. On the other hand, if you stand like an automaton and just beat time, they will soon switch off. Just as singers tend to copy the tone and style they hear around them, so many of them will unconsciously mimic your own movements, so whatever facial expressions or other movements you wish them to make must come from you as you conduct.

If any of your choir move by themselves naturally and unconsciously - perhaps little movements of the head, leaning forward slightly in highly concentrated passages, or even swaying in time a little, do not discourage them. In fact, quite the opposite - you would probably like the rest of the choir to do the same. No matter how perfectly they sing, if your choristers stand there like rows of little woodentops they'll be boring to watch, and your audience has nothing else to look at, has it, once it's read your programme notes three or four times?

One of the most useful exercises we have undertaken recently was to introduce a video camera into rehearsals. A helper slowly panned round the choir as they worked, and later we were able to plug it into a television and watch the results. Although the sound quality wasn't too good, many singers were appalled to see how static their mouths were, how their eyes were wandering all over the room, how visually obvious it was when they took a breath in the wrong place, how they were slouching in their posture etc. And similarly they were able to see for the first time which of their friends had mobile faces, lively eyes and an attractive posture. Then we tried again, and could detect an instant improvement. This one session was more effective than months of nagging.

Summary

- *Power comes from the warmup*

- *Emphasise good posture right from the start and all the time*

- *We can all make the sound we want to make. The trick is knowing what we want*

- *Good tone comes from a lively face, smiling eyes, plenty of air and the ends of the words. Plus a few other things ...*

- *Be very nice to your altos. Be quite tolerant with your second sopranos. Your first sopranos can look after themselves*

- *Sing from memory - just <u>do</u> it!*

- *Diction takes more thought than effort. Concentrate on the ends of words, not the beginnings, and be prepared to cheat*

- *All singing = BREATH IN - BREATH OUT*

- *They can't sing in tune if they can't hear themselves. They can't sing in tune if they can't hear each other*

- *There are lots of "tricks" for singing in tune. Teach your choir to use them, and insist that they do*

- *Communication can be learnt, just like anything else*

INTERMEZZO - THE REDUNDANT CONDUCTOR

Once you've got your choir started and learning, and you are comfortable with what you're doing, it's a good idea to go back and reconsider how best you should direct their performance. It may seem an odd thing to say, but I believe our task is to make ourselves redundant as far as possible, and gently push most of the responsibility for their performance onto them, the singers.

In this way you'll be creating in them a genuine feeling for, and understanding of, the music they sing. You'll be inculcating the calm confidence that comes from them knowing exactly what to do and how to do it. You'll be giving them that wonderful feeling of being part of a team that works together and looks after its members. And by letting them, in a sense, direct you, you will increase the affection and loyalty they feel to you and to the choir.

There are practical benefits, too: you will have a choir that can still perform even if you are incapacitated, and one that will be largely immune to any errors you might make. You may be having a bad day, but that doesn't mean they have to.

Here's how it works ...

Less is more

As your choir get to know their music better and better, be sure always to make the same movements in the same places, but make them *smaller and smaller*.

Particularly once they know their music by memory, you will find that the tiniest motion of finger or eyebrow is sufficient <u>provided they are expecting it</u> – that's why it's so important to do the same thing every time. Whereas at the beginning you made large movements and, as it were, imposed your will on them, now their eyes will come to you for the indications they rely on, and you will start to feel that it is they who are conducting you, and not the other way around.

When this happens it gives you a most satisfying feeling, for it means that you have done your work well. However it's vital that you don't let them down - if they expect a sign from you at a particular place, however tiny it is, make sure they get it every time.

What do I mean by smaller and smaller?

Movements can become very small indeed and still be effective. Sometimes they can actually become more effective – Christopher Adey, the well-known orchestral conductor, once told me that if he thinks an orchestra isn't watching him well enough, he makes his beat much smaller. He believes they are more likely to be attentive when they have to work hard to see what he's doing.

Over the weeks of rehearsal, as the music becomes more and more familiar, you can refine your gestures down and down to mere finger-movements or slight movements of the head; even the odd raised eyebrow can be a significant signal to singers who have been seeing that same eyebrow at the same point with the same meaning for the last three months. Your choir will never lose their concentration, and being able to stand in front of them and direct by hardly moving a muscle will give you a feeling of great satisfaction and power, and what's wrong with that? You thoroughly deserve it, because it comes from careful, consistent and thoughtful rehearsal.

There is one person you can't treat in quite the same way, though, and that's your accompanist. He (or she, of course) is very unlikely to be playing from memory, and therefore can't be watching you every second of the time. On those occasions when he does get the chance to look up at you, he needs to see at the very least a clear and steady beat. He will also look to you for clear indications of changes in tempo, *rallentandi, accelerandi* etc.

I once took a choir to a competition where they were highly amused by the antics of the conductor of one of the other groups. His choir was young, rather small and not strong, but he conducted in great, flamboyant sweeps, his hands at times practically touching the floor, at others flapping wildly. It did his choir no good, of course, simply distracting the attention of the audience and the judges away from his choir's virtues. So minimising your own rôle is probably an excellent thing to aim for. The audience are there to hear your choir, not to watch <u>you</u> showing off!

The automatic choir
Although you should always give your choir the gestures they look for, there are some things that don't need conducting at all. Oddly enough, they are things which most conductors would consider absolutely vital – beginnings and endings!

Try this. Choose a phrase that ends with a long note and a sharp consonant. Practise it a couple of times normally, delicately indicating the consonant by bringing your thumb and fingertips together.

Now make the choir mirror your neat movement by nodding slightly at you as they put the consonant on, and by making an almost imperceptible movement of their hands/elbows/copies. Here you must bully them a bit. Some will not find this a natural thing to do, or feel embarrassed, but they must. Their movement should be very slight, not big enough to distract the audience but big enough that the singers on either side can sense it easily.

Now sing it again, but this time don't conduct the ending – just make the same infinitesimal movement as they do. You'll find that they sing the consonant just as neatly.

Now comes the clever part. Turn your back and make them do it without you. Wonder of wonders, it'll still work (probably; it might take a couple of goes).

Explain to them that they need not look at each other; they can "feel" each other. Telepathy works! In reality they are probably seeing tiny movements out of the corners of their eyes. They should each try to imagine that they are the Head Chorister, responsible for secretly directing everyone else by breath and subtle movements.

It may seem unlikely, but I have found this to work reliably time after time. Make them responsible for all their endings in this way, whether you conduct them or not. This will leave you free to worry about other things. And like you, they will find that in time the physical indications they have to give each other will get smaller and more subtle until they'll reach a point where ... well, who knows? Perhaps telepathy is real after all?

The next step is to apply the same principle to entries as well, and it can work just as well. Choose a piece that has a nice, straightforward *mezzo-forte* entry to practise with. Start by conducting it normally, but be sure to indicate the breath before it, accurately on the beat, by breathing in yourself and letting them see you do it.

Once you are satisfied that they really have taken on board the message that the entry is actually the breath before the sound, and that they are doing this exactly in unison, stop waving your arms about and give them the entry just by breathing in. They'll go with you, no trouble.

Now get them to do the entry without you, by using the "Head Chorister" technique. It won't take long for this to work. Then you can get really clever – make them do the same thing without accompaniment and completely unprepared. This will be harder – the first time, some brave soul will take a big breath and then chicken out and not sing, or perhaps they'll sing and no one will come with them.

<u>Praise this person</u>: they are the one who's done the right thing, and everyone else has let them down. The first person to sing is the winner! - provided they have prepared it properly and given a clear lead.

Make them persevere, and before long you'll find that they can make the entry neatly, 100% together and with no fuss at all. We have done this in competitions – the choir go onto the stage carrying their first notes in their heads, take up the positions they've rehearsed (because we have, of course, practised this almost as much as we have the music), and simply start singing exactly in tune and exactly together. It impresses the socks off everyone and makes the choir feel like a million dollars. If only everyone knew how easy it is to do.

It may seem paradoxical to work in rehearsals to make yourself largely redundant in this way, but if you think about it, it makes a lot of sense. For a large group of singers to make a neat entry or put on a precise little consonant simply by watching the hand-movements of someone standing several yards away from them isn't very likely, is it? Also, you don't want your choir to become so reliant on you that they have to be spoon-fed every entry and every ending. That way they'll never develop a natural sense of timing, and without that, their singing will never be totally precise. Precision cannot be achieved by watching alone: precision needs to be <u>felt</u>.

Every child a conductor

The next step is quite a small one – from your singers conducting each other, to your singers conducting <u>you</u>. Conducting should be a two-way process. It isn't just you telling them what to do and when to do it – <u>they</u> must also tell <u>you</u> when they're going to make an entry, or just how much *rubato* they want to do, or when they're ready to close at the end of a piece.

Ask them to imagine they are "conducting you back" with their heads, their eyes, their faces, their copies, their bodies. As usual their indications need to be small and subtle – this is communication between you and them, not them and the rest of the world. It will help if your own movements are restrained as well – they will tend to naturally mirror what you do.

Your choir will only master this ... what should we call it? Technique? Trick? Perhaps it's more an attitude than anything else? ... if they are very secure in their music. It's a waste of time to even mention it while they are still learning. But in pieces they know well and can sing confidently, you will discover a whole new level of rapport, ensemble and confidence which will overnight transform their performance from good to magical. A choir that can do this with you is a delight to conduct. I suppose you could call it a choir that ... well, conducts itself ...

A bit of fun

In pursuit of this self-confidence and self-determination, there are some enjoyable games you can play. Use them only in conjunction with material they are quite familiar with, and it's usually best if that material is unaccompanied.

My bonny lies over the ocean

First, here is a very silly game that serves no useful purpose at all, except that it introduces a tune which is rather handy for all sorts of experimental activities. It's also an absolute hoot, and children love it. It's a good way to wind down at the end of a rehearsal, or to warm up a class who are coming to you to sing for the first time.

The tune "My bonny lies over the ocean" is well-known, or if they don't know it, it's quickly taught. You might have to tell the younger ones what "bonny" means.

Now, bit by bit, introduce signs to replace some of the words. For instance, "my" and "me" can be a finger pointing at one's own chest. Sing the song, leaving out the "me"s and "my"s and doing the sign instead. Then introduce another sign, say a hand making a wavy shape in the air for "ocean" and "sea", and sing again, leaving out all the "ocean"s, "sea"s, "me"s and "my"s and doing the signs instead.

And so on ... other signs might be ...

> ... "bonny" - a rather rude curvy shape in the air with both hands
>   indicating a female figure ...
> ... "lies" - leaning the head on two clasped hands to suggest sleeping ...
> ... "over" - a high curving shape in the air, pointing away ...
> ... "bring back" - a great big beckoning movement with both hands.

Make the children stand up, and if they sing in the wrong place they have to sit down (but they can still carry on playing). The winner is the last person standing.

Taking turns

It sharpens up concentration if you make them sing in turns. Divide the choir into two halves, and have them sing a song with the first half singing the first line, the second singing the second line, the first half the third line and so on.

Then make them do the same, but musical phrase by musical phrase. At least this will teach them what a phrase is!

Then try it word by word, or bar by bar, or (most difficult) note by note.

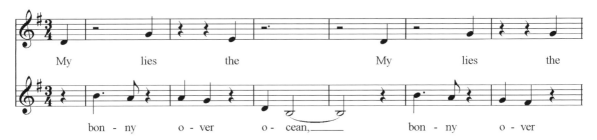

Then divide them up by walking round the choir saying "You're one, you're two, you're one, you're two ..." and so on, so that the two halves end up scrambled.

Singing in a circle

Arrange your choir in a large circle, facing inwards. Invite them to pick someone roughly opposite to them on the other side of the circle to be their "target".

Then get them to sing, all together, some piece from their repertoire that they know pretty well. Make them sing it quite unconducted, using their "telepathy" trick to start together.

Their aim must be to focus their sound, their facial and bodily movements, their diction and all their attention on their "target" across the circle. Tell them to see if they can't put their target singer off, or embarrass them or make them laugh. Yes, it can be quite a nasty game, especially if several of them have chosen the same person as their target! They'll think it's great fun, however.

The object, as you will have guessed, is to get them used to projecting their performance outwards, and to give them confidence in their attitudes, posture and expression. It's useful to explain to them that while their performance may have an off-putting effect on their target, that's only true because the target is still quite close to them, and he or she knows they are a target and knows what to expect. When they do the same thing to an audience the distance will be greater, the effect ameliorated, and all the audience will know is that they are listening to a choir that displays a lively self-confidence and is at all times interesting to watch.

Later you could try dividing the choir into two or three groups so that the circle is smaller and the effects more immediate. If they seem to be enjoying it (as I'm sure they will) the ultimate would be to pit two children against each other and see who's the first to cave in!

Taking the music for a walk

None of these games will transform your choir's singing at one fell stroke. At the very least, though, they will make your rehearsals much more fun, and at most they will gradually make your choristers confident in their own ability to perform in public, and remove all trace of embarrassment and diffidence in the face of an audience. Let's face it, singing to an audience is probably a great deal less scary than singing to your own friends and fellow choir members.

Choose a piece they know well, preferably in two or more parts and preferably unaccompanied, and make them "take it for a walk". Clear the chairs out of the way so they have as big a space as possible, set them off singing, and lead them slowly round the room, singing as they go. Follow a serpentine path so the head of the column passes close to the tail from time to time.

Then tell them to keep walking and singing, but to go wherever they like, each wandering round the room in a random fashion. Keeping their minds on their singing, their posture, their facial expression and diction as well as looking where they are going may be quite a challenge – what we're trying to do is make all those things become automatic so they'll do them without thinking. Passing by and among others who are singing different parts will also make them more secure on their own part by listening hard for their own line and paying less attention to the others.

Later you could invite them to "go for a walk" until they find a friend who they can hear is singing a different part, and go for a walk with them as a pair. If they're girls, you can suggest they might hold hands as they go; if they're boys, perhaps not!

In my own rehearsals I combine this game with a little practice at spacing themselves to sing. Once in a while as they walk, I call out that they should get as far away from anyone else as they can, and keep singing all the while. Then I get them to slowly walk into the centre of the room so they form a dense crowd, with the parts all jumbled up, still singing. We have a little discussion about "Which feels most comfortable, singing miles away from everyone else, or standing close?"

Older singers especially seem to prefer standing apart, and if the acoustic of a concert-hall or church allows, it's sometimes good to do this in a concert. I have known outstanding performances where the children stood a good six feet apart, and it certainly looks very impressive and professional. Obviously this only works in a very large building or on a very large stage, and you'll have to judge whether the acoustical properties of the building will prevent them from hearing each other, or will attenuate the sound so the effect is weedy.

Giving themselves a concert

When we have plenty of rehearsal time, usually shortly before a concert so the music is all well known, we sometimes let the choir divide themselves into small groups and choose a piece from the repertoire to sing to the rest of the choir. You'll obviously have to make sure that no one gets left out like the little fat boy who's always the last to be picked at football, and you also need to ensure that every group has enough people on each part.

My experience has been that they enjoy this very much, and that they are extremely supportive and appreciative of each other's performance. As in all these activities, we are seeking to increase the singers' self-confidence and self-reliance. If one ever reached the stage where the choir really doesn't need to be conducted at all, I'd say that was a job well done. As any orchestral conductor will tell you, if he's doing his job properly 90% of his work takes place in rehearsal, and only 10% in the concert.

Antiphonal singing and "special effects"

When you reach the enviable position of having a choir that can do all these things with accuracy and aplomb, you could start thinking about startling your audience with some special effects.

There are some songs that invite antiphonal singing – two groups somewhat apart, singing either against each other or by turns. The most obvious example is found in church choirs which for generations past have been accustomed to divide themselves on each side of the chancel; one half is usually known as "decani" and the other as "cantoris". Though most of the time they sing as one, there are parts of a church service when they may be divided, such as the psalms or canticles which can be chanted verse and verse about.

Of course each half of the choir needs to be self-sufficient and balanced in terms of strength, confidence and numbers to each part.

If you can find, or arrange yourself, works that allow this type of singing, you should bear in mind that the dry acoustic of most concert halls, theatres and school halls makes it less effective. It's a trick that works best in the "loose" acoustic (in other words, with a tiny bit of echo) of a church, and even then you'll need to set rehearsal time aside to experiment. I have know churches where it worked stunningly well, and others where it was a disaster. Somehow you can never tell which it'll be until you get the choir in there and actually try it out.

Variations on this can be fascinating. There are a few works (Britten's *Hymn to the Virgin* is an obvious example, and very beautiful indeed but only suitable for youth choirs as it's SATB) that have a semi-chorus – a small group of singers set aside but usually including all the parts, perhaps two or three singers to each. Mysterious and beautiful effects can be achieved by experimenting with the placement of the semi-chorus. It might even be possible to put them completely out of sight of the audience, and if they are skilled at directing themselves they could be out of sight of the conductor as well.

The difficulty will always lie in finding the right repertoire, or adapting what you do find. I went as far myself as writing a whole set of pieces especially for the purpose. They're called "Four Corners of the Building" and are available from the Choirmaster Press (www.choirmaster.co.uk) in both upper-voice and SATB versions, but be warned – they're pretty hard and only suitable for a fairly advanced choir.

Extract from "Four Corners of the Building" (SSA+SSA)

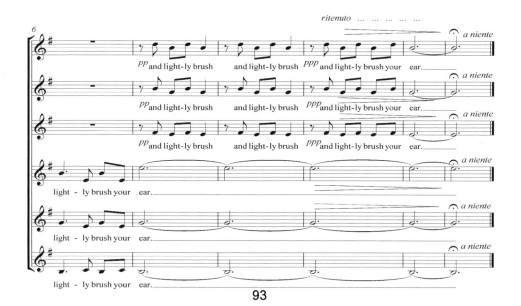

RECAPITULATION - YOUR CHOIR IN PERFORMANCE

When and where to sing - finding performance opportunities

Sooner or later you'll be asked to sing out of doors, at a school fête or something like that. The choir will sound weedy in the open air, the singers won't enjoy it because they won't be able to hear each other very well and they'll feel exposed, and although the audience may still like it because, let's face it, everyone likes to see young people perform, musically it will be a non-event. Don't do it.

Unless you are running a church choir which exists for the specific purpose of providing music for regular worship, you will have a problem finding audiences. Concert audiences are not enormous at the best of times, and a choir doesn't seem to have the same pulling-power as an orchestra, however good it is. You will have a certain captive audience, of course - the mums and dads, aunties and grandpas who will come to everything you do, bless them. But usually these only amount to about two or at best three per choir-member, which won't fill a hall.

Nor is publicity the answer. I am often asked "Why don't you put more adverts in the local papers, you'd get big audiences then?" but I have to answer "No, we wouldn't. Year after year we've sent out press releases, talked to the local radio, sent out recordings, put adverts in the papers, distributed posters to all the local schools, libraries and churches. You name it, we've tried it - and on the whole it hasn't worked". Sadly, this is quite true. Fifty posters and a great big (and very expensive) advert in the paper might bring you another half-a-dozen people in the audience if you're lucky.

Local newspapers are frustrating to deal with. In my experience they are profoundly indifferent to the things that interest us. Our local papers totally ignored a press release that told them "Two hundred and fifty local youngsters travel to Budapest at the invitation of the British Embassy to represent Great Britain by giving a total of twelve concerts" (we did, too - we took a youth orchestra, a wind band, the choir and a small string orchestra all at once). No doubt it would have been a different matter if they had been able to print "Conductor falls off stage - twelve-year-old violinist crushed"!

In fact in July 2000 we had ample proof of this when one of our ensembles was *en route* to the hotel destroyed in the tragic Concorde accident near Paris. The national press showed an intense and morbid interest in us for a short time, but were of course only concerned to get sensational pictures of distraught children. As we were in fact nowhere near the accident and knew little about it, we were a bit of a disappointment to them.

Nevertheless, you have to try, and keep trying. Find out who the News Editor of your local newspaper is, and send him a neat, short, double-spaced typewritten press release every time you do something interesting, including your phone number if he wants to know anything, and an offer of a photo-opportunity. He is much more likely to use it if you can give him some human (or animal) interest - "Sweet ickle kitten, missing for three months, found asleep in choir's music box", "Nine-year-old soprano peels 17 million potatoes to raise funds for choir trip" or "White slaver Head Master sells children to buy choir minibus" might do the trick. Just saying "this is a really good choir and it's got local children in it" won't wash at all.

I have had more luck with local radio. Find out if there's a daytime "housewives and pensioners"-type programme, send them a press release and offer to sing carols for them to record at Christmas time. If they ask you for an interview, turn up on time with a piece of paper on which you have jotted down everything you wish to say, especially the date, time, place and cost of your next concert. Without this, it'll all fly out of your head at the wrong moment.

If you have sponsors, see if they have access to good publicity-routes. When going abroad our local youth orchestra used to get a very cheap deal from a local van-hire firm, and a free passage for the instrument van from a ferry company that happened to be based locally. Because they placed a lot of very expensive advertising with local newspapers they were sometimes able to excite more interest than the orchestra could manage for itself. Sadly this sort of thing is largely a thing of the past, though: these days businesses are strapped for cash, and the influence of television has diverted sponsorship money away to anything involving "celebrities", or daft sponsored events for charity.

However good your publicity, getting good big audiences will always be a problem. One effective solution is to ally yourself with another organisation. For several years we gave an annual concert for a well-organised local charity. They booked our largest concert-hall and looked after all the publicity, ticket-sales and front-of-house, and we simply provided the musical content. Because they had their own network of contacts and their own "captive audience" who turned out to support not the choir but the charity, we always got a full house.

We also give two or three concerts each year in local churches. It's very convenient to be running a choir and not an orchestra, because church acoustics suit us very well and we don't need an enormous amount of space. In practical terms the only difficulty is that we have to use an electric piano instead of a proper one, though they are awfully good these days.

In a sense we are able to make the church an offer it can't afford to refuse. We give them a good two-hour concert, for which we require them to (a) if necessary provide some simple staging for the choir to stand on, usually borrowed from a local school, (b) provide adequate lighting, (c) pay us a fee which we use to hire a coach to get the children there, and (d) give the children their tea in the church hall in between the rehearsal and the concert - there are always ladies in the church congregation who are good at this.

For their part, they can charge what they like for admission and they get to keep any profit. It's a good deal for everyone. We get a "free" concert venue and a nice afternoon out, with a good audience at the end because it's in the church's own interest to get as many "bums on seats" as possible. The church has a fund-raising opportunity at very little risk, and at very little trouble to themselves compared with their usual jumble-sales and church teas.

If yours is not a school choir but a privately-organised group, consider making a similar offer to a school - perhaps one from which you draw several pupils. They might welcome your participation in a school concert, so they don't have to provide so much music themselves. They are unlikely to be able or willing to pay a "fee", but a useful spin-off is that quite a number of young potential members will hear you.

Similarly, look for other musical ensembles that cannot manage a concert all by themselves and propose a concert-share. Perhaps there is a local children's or youth orchestra that has half a programme of music prepared and will welcome your offer to provide the other half. In that way, both of you will benefit from the other's captive audience of parents etc. Other adult groups may also like to offer you a short "spot" in one of their concerts. If your local choral society or adult orchestra can be persuaded to do so, you will profit from their audience and are almost certain to be a hit because of the youth and enthusiasm of your performers. People love to see and hear children perform, and a young choir of any quality can often put adults in the shade - tough on the adults but a welcome boost to your morale.

Round Christmas time groups like yours are in some demand, although the circumstances under which you will be required to perform may not be ideal. Shopping malls like to have children singing carols during the day, and hospitals and old people's homes may welcome a short recital. However, it means dedicating quite a lot of rehearsals to learning Christmas music you can't perform for the rest of the year, so I'm not very keen myself.

Whatever arrangement you make with an outside organisation, especially if you are entering a "contract" (however informal) with a charity or church, do put it in writing. Discuss it first, and then send them a letter saying exactly what you undertake to do for them (how many singers, what sort of music, whether you will provide the programmes or not, how long the concert will be etc.) and what you expect them to do for you (provide the venue, pay you a fee or expenses, organise staging, lighting, food etc.). Say you know they would prefer that everyone know exactly where they stand, and ask them to confirm the agreement in writing. I have done this for years, and have only had one dispute. On that occasion, it was useful to be able to take out the correspondence and say "Ah, but look, you promised ...."

In planning your performance programme, avoid making your choir and its normal working methods subservient to other activities. It's all too easy to let your choir become a convenience to others in the guise of providing them with "opportunities". Beware the choral society conductor who phones up saying "Would your girls like to sing with us in our next concert? It'll be good experience for them". Actually, he is very short of sopranos and altos and is hoping you will help him out. And it probably won't be good experience for them, either. Most adult choral societies work far too slowly for children's impatient minds and quick intelligence, and I have found some choral society members look down their noses at young singers in the mistaken belief that because they have sung *Messiah* thirty-seven times they are somehow more experienced and better singers (whereas, to be honest, the opposite is often the case).

Of course, if the conductor phoned up and said "We're doing Britten's *St.Nicholas* and we'd like you to be the Gallery Choir" (or perhaps the children's choir section in *Carmina Burana*) that would be a different matter. In that case you would be going in, probably for the last two or three rehearsals and the performance, as "guest artists". You would be personally responsible for teaching the music, and you would remain in control until the last minute. Also, your performance will stand on its own merits and if the adult chorus turns out to be a disaster, your choir won't necessarily share in the disgrace. Of course, if they turn out to be really good and your children don't know their notes .....! Resist attempts to make the children turn up to more rehearsals than you consider absolutely necessary, and do read the section below about "singing with an orchestra".

If yours is a school choir you are almost certain to be expected to provide "just one song for assembly" - which you can easily do, and probably should do, sometimes. But if you do it every week, the idea and the singing will become stale. Your choir must always be made to feel that they, and what they do, are the most important thing - and very special. So try to impress on your Head Teacher that the choir should be reserved for really special occasions. Fortunately in dealing with Head Teachers you have a great advantage in that you offer them a really good "shop window" activity, something that delights and impresses parents and prospective parents and will attract pupils to the school. Most Heads realise this.

Similarly, be cautious about involvement with the other arts. This may seem selfish, but in my experience when you include some singing in a school play or dance activity for instance, it is always the demands of the acting, the production or the dance that are the most important - possibly because you and your choir work together regularly, have your act together and are therefore the least "trouble". Again, your choir is too important to be relegated to the background for something else.

All your decisions about choir performances should be based only on the needs of the choir and its members (the most important people), their parents (quite important too) and yourself (also quite important!). Ask yourself these questions:

> "Will this performance benefit the choir?"
> "Will the choir-members enjoy it?"
> "Will they learn anything from it?"
> "And do I, myself, <u>want</u> to do it?"

Unless the answer includes at least two "yesses", forget it.

Choral competitions

Competitive festivals are popular with children's choirs, and I am very much in favour of them.

Philosophically many musicians are opposed to the idea of using music as a competitive sport, and you will be at the mercy of judges and adjudicators whose ideas and judgements may differ wildly from your own. All the same, in my experience it can be very beneficial to you and your singers to hear other choirs and be able to judge just how well you are doing in comparison, and children usually enjoy it very much. They are tremendously competitive and will take their rehearsals and performance far more seriously than for a boring old concert. When they win, the boost in confidence, morale and enthusiasm is colossal. When they lose, they're surprisingly philosophical about it.

The most important benefit to your singers comes from hearing other choirs that are not as good as they are (and trust me, there are <u>always</u> choirs that aren't as good as they are). Sure, you've told them how well they're doing – but you would, wouldn't you? Their parents and family have praised them, too – but <u>they</u> would as well. But to sit in the audience and hear with their own ears and see with their own eyes that they really are good ... well, that makes all the difference. They'll go home feeling ten feet tall; the effect will last and last.

If you are entering a local festival or competition, do some research in advance. Will the class you have chosen have enough entrants to be worthwhile? I once entered a festival to find that we were the only choir in the class, which seemed a little pointless. Will you get to hear other choirs like yours, or are all the classes mixed up? Again, I entered the local heats of "Music for Youth" and found that each session included entrants in a number of different classes. Although it was nice to hear a school orchestra, recorder groups, string quartet etc., what we actually wanted to hear was other choirs like ours.

Check, too, that you are entering a class where you won't be treading unfairly on other people's toes. I know one festival where the senior choir section consists entirely of little groups of elderly ladies from the local Women's Institutes. I am sure that a largish, well-trained, experienced, fresh and lively young choir could win without difficulty, but where's the profit in that? And would it be fair?

Nationally our most important contest, the "Choir of the Year", happens every other year. It used to be sponsored by Sainsbury's and was run very efficiently. The semi-finals and finals were televised by the BBC, and made compelling viewing. Sadly Sainsbury's pulled out and the BBC decided to run it themselves. My experience was that it was not nearly such a good or enjoyable competition under the BBC's management.

The massive, high-profile "Music for Youth" Festival is annual, and the address is Music for Youth, 3rd Floor, South Wing, Somerset House, Strand, London WC2R 1LA . It offers the opportunity of performing on London's South Bank and, if you're very good, at the Royal Albert Hall. It is possible to skip the first round and send a taped entry instead, but I have not had much luck doing this. The organisers say that choirs sending taped entries have just as much chance of being selected for the main festival as those that travel to the regional heats but I'm not sure, for instance, how they can judge from a tape the quality of a choir's stage presence and presentation.

Also every two years is the National Choir Competition which is held at Peterborough. This is a friendly, well-run event and highly recommended, although only in the all-comers Championship Class do standards even begin to approach those of "Choir of the Year".

To find out about other competitive festivals you need to join The British Federation of Festivals for Music, Dance and Speech (Festivals House, 198 Park Lane, Macclesfield, Cheshire SK11 6UD tel. 01625 428297). Non-competitive festivals up and down the country (most of them for professional musicians, unfortunately) are also listed in a special annual supplement to *"Classical Music"* magazine, published by Rhinegold.

In any competition, presentation is at least as important as musical excellence, so ...

- Always sing from memory. If possible, you should conduct from memory too.

- Try to get a look at the venue beforehand, so you arrive knowing the layout of the hall and of the stage. Make a particular note of the toilets; little girls especially seem to have little bladders, and can't sing their best with their legs crossed. Build toilet time into your preparations.

- Practise thoroughly how your choir is going to get on and off the stage. Every singer must know exactly where he or she will stand, and this means inventing some system of orientation. My own method is to appoint one singer whose task is to go on first, and position herself exactly in the middle of the stage. The others then follow on and place themselves in relation to her. See the next section.

- Don't be tempted to show how perfectionist you are, and how excellent your control over your choir, by standing in front of them making little adjustments to their positions. You should have done all that during rehearsal. It's amateurish and impresses no one.

- There is some argument about whether you should wait until the adjudicator indicates that he or she is ready before you begin. Personally I wait until I get a nod from the adjudicator before starting the first song, but thereafter I don't hang about moving from one song to the next. I believe that good manners and the convenience of the adjudicator should take second place to your need to present a well-planned programme that flows easily.

- The behaviour of your choir while others are singing is also important. I have encountered some unbelievably inconsiderate behaviour – talking, running about, making loud comments etc. - fortunately from only a minority of choirs.

- DO warm your choir up beforehand, if necessary taking them outside to do so. But DON'T try to use the time before the competition starts to have an extra rehearsal. This is amateurish and smacks of panic. Plan everything beforehand – so long to get off the coach and into the building, so long for the children to change, so long to go to the toilet, so long for the warm-up etc. Don't rush the children, and don't let them rush about either. You are being watched (by the other choirs) right from the moment you get off the bus; the more calm and confident you and your choir appear, the less confident the opposition will be.

● Never contest the result of a competition. The judging isn't always perfect and not all adjudicators are terribly expert. On the other hand no adjudicator, however expert, will ever see your little darlings in quite the same rosy light as you. Put up, shut up and try to learn what it was the winning choirs did that you did not.

Getting on and getting off again

I'll discuss this here because it's especially important in choral competitions, though of course it applies to all performances.

I cannot emphasise too strongly that how your choir gets on and off the stage is vitally important. It's the one time when everyone is watching them with keen curiosity and no music to distract them, and it's your choir's opportunity to impress with their calm professionalism and buoyant self-confidence. A competition adjudicator may not really be allowed to take it into account in his judgement, but it's hard to ignore and can certainly influence the final result.

The job needs to be done neatly and with no fuss at all. The very last thing you want is children wandering around not knowing where they're supposed to be. It also needs to be quick: when I've been working as an adjudicator it's hard to express the tedium of some large (usually adult) choirs plodding carefully and slowly one by one onto the stage, row after row until you wonder if it's ever going to end. What we are after is an impression that the stage is one moment empty, the next moment filled with singers poised and ready to sing.

Obviously there are lots of ways to accomplish the desired effect, but I'll offer my own solution in case it might be helpful ...

Let's suppose that the choir is going to stand in three gently curved rows. Naturally you want the taller ones at the back. I am lucky that we are usually able to sing with the parts scrambled so the children can arrange themselves strictly by height without having to worry about who is standing next to who. The choir arrange themselves round the room in a long crocodile with the tallest at the front and the shortest at the back. Then we start creating the back row by making the tallest child go to one end, the next tallest to the other end, the next to the first end, the next to the second end and so on until the row is complete. Then we fill the second row in the same way, and lastly the front row. So we end up with the tallest row at the back, with its very tallest members at each end. The shortest children of all will be in the centre of the front row so their mums can see them easily and say "Aah, aren't they sweet!"

This arrangement is done before the first concert of the season, and usually lasts the season through.

We then appoint the middle child in the back row as the "middle marker". The centre <u>two</u> children in the second row are the "middle markers" for their row, and the centre child in the front is the marker for that row.

Before the concert or competition I make sure that the back row middle marker knows exactly where he or she is going to stand, if possible by going on to the stage and practising. Then at the beginning of the performance, all we have to do is send the back row middle marker on to station themselves at that spot. The rest of the back row follow quickly on – not even necessarily in the right order – and range themselves on either side, spaced out and curved as they've previously practised.

They are followed by the two middle markers of the second row who stand in front of and to either side of the back row middle, and the second row enter and take their places.

Finally the middle marker of the front row leads in and places him or herself in the centre, and the job's done.

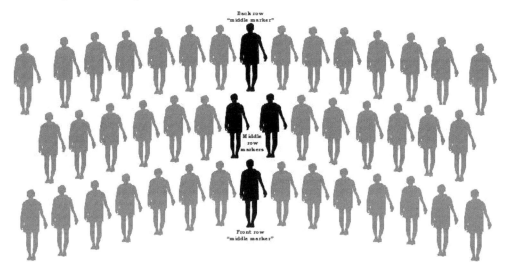

At the end of the concert the process is reversed – the front row middle marker leads off, followed by the rest of the front row, then the second row and then the back row. As the front row middle marker is one of the youngest, it's as well to station an adult nearby to make sure he or she doesn't get lost on the way back to the dressing room.

The advantage of this scheme is that it doesn't matter whether the choir have to enter stage left, stage right, or up some steps at the front: the process is always exactly the same, and they can do it it any building and any space at the drop of a hat. As they have practised it beforehand, and because it never varies from concert to concert, they always know exactly where to go and there's no fussing or uncertainty. It doesn't even matter if the rows don't enter in the right order; each child can find his or her place quickly and it still looks neat. Above all, it's quick and you don't keep the audience waiting.

One further thing to impress on your singers: the moment they enter the hall, they are on display and people are watching and judging. Many of the audience may not know much about music, but they know what they can see. Whether it's a concert or a competition, there's no point in losing any opportunity to make a good impression.

How to organise a foreign tour, and where to go

Increasingly in the last few years it has become the "done thing" for choirs and other ensembles to undertake concert-tours abroad. The advantages are several - audiences can be better than at home and frequently much more enthusiastic, one finds some truly remarkable and beautiful concert venues, and one is giving the young members of the choir an experience they will never forget. Quite apart from the scenery and the concerts, one finds a corporate spirit and camaraderie developing that takes them all home again on an emotional "high". So here are a few tips ......

Don't try and organise the thing yourself. Use a firm of professional tour-promoters like Club Europe, NST or Rayburn. They will find and book accommodation, ferries, coaches, concerts etc. and will be responsible for your publicity. They will send a professional courier to look after you as well, and if things go wrong they are big enough and experienced enough to sort it out. Such firms are very familiar with the needs of groups like yours, and will often have "off-the-peg" tours that will suit you very well - a residence and set of venues that have been used by other groups in the past so that you will be following a well-worn and well-organised path. These firms regularly send their advertising brochures to practically every school in the country, so it shouldn't be too hard tracking them down. Or once again, try the *Music Education Yearbook* or the internet.

Make the assumption that you are all going abroad to work. You don't want a week's holiday with two concerts thrown in; stress to your tour arrangers that you want at least four concerts and not more than one free day, if indeed you have a free day at all. The devil makes work for idle hands to do, and your singers will be at their happiest doing what they do best, so keep them busy. However, you should not assume that you will be able to do much meaningful rehearsal while abroad. Most hotels and hostels cannot provide a suitable room in which to work, and although you should expect a one- or two-hour rehearsal in the venue before each concert, this will mostly be taken up with things like "where do we stand?", "how do we get on and off the stage?" and "what order are we singing the songs in?" rather than real musical rehearsal. Get all your music thoroughly learnt before you go.

One of the most pressing reasons for going abroad is to find really good, enthusiastic audiences. We have encountered excellent audiences in Italy, Hungary, Poland, Spain and France, adequate ones in Switzerland and Austria, mediocre ones in Germany and Holland, and downright pathetic in Belgium. That said, a lot depends on your publicity - if your tour promoters and their local representatives are on the ball, they will get you on posters, local newspapers and radio and will drum up a good crowd for you. This is truest in France where, in stark contrast to England, posters work very well. Malta's supposed to be good, but I've never been there with a choir because of the expensive air fare. Concert venues that are really hot tourist-spots can produce very large audiences indeed. We once had an estimated three-and-a-half thousand in Notre Dame Cathedral in Paris - but they were mostly trippers who came in during the concert, sat and listened for a bit and then drifted out again to be replaced by some more. These days I prefer concerts in small towns that don't get much live music. Audiences may be numbered in one or two hundreds instead of thousands, but they do love it so!

Consider your travel arrangements carefully. Most musical ensembles travel by coach and ferry because this is by far the cheapest option. However even from the South of England, only Northern and Central France, Belgium, Holland and the nearest part of Germany can really be reached in one day. If you wish to go any further you will have to travel for two days there and two days back. Your tour company will press you to travel overnight and sleep on the coach which will save the cost of an overnight hotel/hostel, but you will arrive tired and cranky. I would always avoid this. Naturally enough it affects the staff more than the youngsters, but your staff are important too! Very few choirs find rail- or air-travel an economic alternative.

Ask your tour company about an inspection trip. This will be a large extra expense to add to the bill, but the advantages are considerable. It is wonderful to be able to tell parents "yes, I've visited the residence and the toilets are clean and the beds are comfortable and the rooms lock at night, and the food is not all frogs' legs, horse-meat and snails ....." and so on. And for you there is considerable comfort in having visited the concert venues and talked to the people about where the toilets are, where the changing room is, whether the light will be adequate and whether the priest minds you singing three-part arrangements of old Sex Pistols hits in his church .....

Be aware that in some continental countries it is common for concerts to start (and therefore end) quite late. In France, for instance, 8.30p.m. is normal, and even then concerts are never expected to actually start on time. In Spain it is not unknown for concerts to be advertised for 10.30 or even 11.00p.m., and then start as much as 45 minutes late! Probably most of your concerts will be in churches, many of which are very beautiful indeed. Most will be Roman Catholic churches and sometimes, though with increasing rarity, you may find that they are not willing for you to perform secular music which is something to think about. Also there is nothing for people to do during an interval, so if you take the normal British break of twenty minutes or so you may find your audience evaporating. Often a 50- or 60-minute concert with no interval is better.

Audiences abroad can often be less formal than at home. In France particularly it is normal for people to wander round the church during a concert, and for some to get up and leave halfway through to be replaced by latecomers. And while at home we usually start and end a concert without any speech-making, on the continent a welcoming speech by a local priest or civic dignitary is common, and you may be expected to speak to the audience as well - "Good evening, we are the Nether Wallop Children's Chorale and tonight we are going to sing for you ....". If you aren't up to doing this, try and get your courier to do it for you from a script you've prepared.

You will find that most concerts are free - it is rare to be able to charge for entrance, especially in churches. We usually take a glossy programme with us, nicely printed with information about the Choir and its music all translated into the appropriate language. We are happy to give them away for nothing because we want people to know about us, but once or twice have been surprised when the audience lined up at the end of the concert to hand their programmes in again! Sweet, really.

Large Catholic churches will sometimes ask you to perform in a Mass. In some places this is the price for being allowed to use the building for a concert. In this case you will probably need to prepare a *Kyrie, Gloria, Sanctus, Benedictus* and *Agnus Dei*, plus one or two short anthems. Don't bother with a *Credo* - you won't need it. Be sure to establish well beforehand whether your accompanist will be expected to play (maybe on the organ?) or if the resident organist will do it, and if the latter, try and get some idea whether he or she is up to the job! Also, be careful that you understand the church's expectations. We once arrived at a church to have some music thrust into our hands which they expected us to learn and sing that morning!

Press your tour company to avoid large youth hostels in major cities. On the continent these are usually secure, comfortable and well-organised. Sometimes they are too well-organised. In Frankfurt we were woken each morning by a voice over the tannoy that barked "Wake up! It is eight o'clock! Get up NOW! Go downstairs and EAT YOUR BREAKFAST!"

However in the summer they can be crowded and noisy places with a fairly mature clientele who keep late hours and can be a little daunting to children and your adult colleagues. Also, avoid cheap hotels in large cities where you can sometimes find yourselves rubbing shoulders with some fairly dubious local characters - of both sexes, if you catch my drift! Infinitely preferable are budget hotels in small towns, youth hostels in small towns, "municipal" hostels such as the Centres d'Accueil in France, and university halls of residence.

Security at night is a major issue for groups like ours, especially in the light of one or two tragic events involving English schoolchildren in recent years. Check that your residence is locked at night, and that there is a member of staff on duty at all times. If the children's bedrooms can be locked, adopt a policy about whether they should lock themselves in at night or not; in general I'd say not, in case of emergencies, but I and my helpers have often sat up at the end of the corridor, keeping watch until the small hours: impress on your staff the need for constant vigilance and especially constant presence. Large groups of girls in particular seem to act like a magnet for undesirable locals in most countries! When I ran a large mixed youth choir, we made a point of mixing up the accommodation so that there were boys' rooms among the girls' on every corridor, in the hope that this would deter intruders. Not that it was ever put to the test; our experience during many years of such trips has been excellent and provided everyone is sensible and thinks ahead you should have no problems. Frankly, most continental cities are a good deal safer than those at home.

If your town has a twinning organisation, by all means use it – you may have a warm and friendly experience. However, "home-stay" arrangements (where individual children are put up in local people' houses) may save money but they can be very upsetting to your tender young flowers who really want to be together with their friends. Never underestimate the importance of young people's social life. Adolescents are at the stage in their lives where they are learning how to form groups and interact within them, and just for the moment their friendships (however short-lived and transitory they seem to us) are the most important thing in the world.

Running mostly girls' choirs I have noticed an odd phenomenon during foreign tours. When they first board the bus, your choir are typical teenagers, streetwise, sassy and very grown up. As the week progresses, they seem to get younger. Teddy-bears make an appearance in bedrooms and on the coach, they tend to giggle a lot and walk round holding hands. It's rather endearing, and fortunately has no effect on the way they do their job.

Your coach driver can be a valuable ally. Make a point of chatting to him, take his advice about routes and journey times, include him as a member of your team, involve him in social activities and generally make him feel important.

Thinking of money, if you imagine an all-in cost (transport, courier, concert arrangements, full-board accommodation) in the region of £70 per person per night, you won't be far out (2010 prices). Naturally the cost varies considerably from company to company and country to country.

Do opt for a full-board arrangement, even though in most cases that will mean that one of the three meals each day will be a rather boring picnic from the canteen at your residence. You might save money by agreeing to go half-board, but the difficulties of making your own arrangements for the whole choir for one meal a day in a strange country are too great to contemplate.

Be sure that your tour company know how many vegetarians you have in the party, and that they have made a point of catering for them. Although it's getting better very quickly, in some European countries especially Poland, Hungary and Czechoslovakia, vegetarianism is not as common as it is in Britain and some restaurants and residences are slap-dash in their provision for it - vegetarian soup made with meat stock, for instance! I well remember one year in Belgium, a country where normally the food is excellent, finding myself in front of the chef shouting "A fish is NOT a vegetable!" Funny in retrospect, but not at the time.

Your responsibilities on such a trip will be enormous - you must be *in loco parentis* and you have a legal obligation to take all reasonable steps to secure the safety and well-being of your young members. You need a good, big team of sensible people with you - not necessarily teachers, for parents are often towers of strength - and you must all be prepared to be "on duty" practically twenty-four hours a day.

For your concerts you're going to need a keyboard. Electric pianos by Yamaha and Roland sound fantastic and are lovely to play on. Buy or borrow the biggest you can afford and carry - they're heavy so you need a couple of dads or a sack-barrow. You'll also need a continental adaptor and a couple of very long extension leads, because in some foreign buildings electricity sockets are few and far between - trust me, I've been there!

If all this sounds a bit daunting, take heart. Concert-tours can be delightful experiences. I love them, have taken part in and organised more than two dozen such trips for different groups, and never regretted a single one.

How to organise a choir concert

Assuming that you are giving a concert on your own without the involvement of other ensembles, your concert should be shorter rather than longer. Be very strict with yourself when choosing music, and time each piece allowing about one minute in each case for applause, finding the next page etc. Aim for a first half of about 40 minutes, followed by a 20 minute interval (intervals are almost never shorter than this - it takes so long for the audience to wander out of their seats and then wander back again), and a 30 minute second half. It's important to send your audience away wanting more, rather than feeling that they spent the last fifteen minutes thinking how uncomfortable the chairs were.

Your choir will need an interval so they can relax, move around after all that standing still, take the weight off their feet and, most importantly, sort out their music for the second half. Because young choirs typically sing a lot of short pieces rather than one or two long ones, the sheer weight of the music can make it impossible for them to carry the whole concert at once. Singing from memory is always better, of course. Incidentally, some poor child almost always drops their music. Deal with this before it happens by telling them not to make a big issue of it and not to grovel round on the floor picking it up, but calmly share with the person next to them.

Do prepare an encore - something short, light and fun. And having prepared it, try to use it. Your singers will be cross with you if you don't. If necessary, prime one or two extrovert dads to stand at the back and shout "Encore! Encore!"

Rather than perform a long succession of short pieces, I group them in twos or threes in the programme according to age, subject matter, country of origin, style or what have you, and perform them as sets. If you have a work that is longer and more weighty than the rest, a good place for it is just before the interval. The end of the concert needs to be upbeat and lively, of course, unless your choir is so good that you can get away with something restrained, sentimental and totally beautiful that will reduce the mums to tears (and I have known it happen - if you want a real tear-jerker, try Bob Chilcott's *Can you hear me?* or Alan Simmons' *All you were and all you are*).

Seventy minutes of choral music is quite a lot, so if possible it is nice to relieve it by including one or two instrumental items. There are always ambitious young musicians looking for their first opportunity to star in a solo rôle. The conductor of your local youth orchestra might be able to point you in the right direction, and so might local violin teachers, flute teachers etc. It is not usually necessary or appropriate to pay them, but do make a fuss of them, treat them as honoured guests however young they are, send their parents complimentary tickets and give them their own potted biography in the programme. Six or seven minutes in each half of the concert seems about right.

Some choir conductors make a habit of talking to the audience, explaining the background of the choir and then introducing each piece. If you are an accomplished public speaker - succinct, confident, loud and humorous - I suppose that's all right. Sadly, we do not all have that gift, and most of us prefer to produce a proper concert programme and thus avoid any need to speak to the audience. After all, professional concerts (in the UK at least - things are different abroad) never begin with a speech. Concert programmes can be produced quite cheaply and look very smart in these days of word-processors, desktop publishing and photocopiers. If you do not have this kind of skill or equipment, I bet you know someone who has - one of the children's fathers, perhaps. The lovely thing about computer enthusiasts is that they are always willing to show you how clever they are!

Programmes should include a paragraph or two about the choir (including how to join, because there may be some potential recruits in the audience), a three- or four-sentence biography of any soloists, a list of your choir's names and some credit to your accompanist, a little panel at the back advertising your next concert, and a brief note about each piece. These programme notes should be short and light-hearted, and not too erudite. The audience really doesn't want to know exactly when the composer died, where he lived (unless he was local), who he studied with etc. They are far more interested to know roughly what the song is about, why it sounds like it does and whether you enjoy singing it!

Here are a few of our old ones to give you the idea:

Love is come again ... ... **Trad. arr. Bardos**
Homage to Bach   ... ... **Somorjai**
St.Gregory's Day   ... ... **Trad.arr.Kodaly**
During our concert-tour to Hungary last year we made contact with several Hungarian choirs and their directors, and were able to "borrow" some repertoire from them. Love is come again is an old French melody, but this arrangement is very popular with Hungarian upper-voice choirs. Homage to Bach, a modern song without words but with its tongue in its cheek, recalls a past epoch. St.Gregory's Day is half in Latin and half in English and paints a rumbustious picture of village life.

Shine out, great sun   ... ... **Handel**
On a poet's lips I slept ... ... **Bairstow**
Two songs from English composers - although Handel was actually German, he lived and worked in this country so long and had such a profound effect on its music that many consider him English by adoption! This beautiful unison aria comes from his dramatic work Samson. Edward Bairstow was well-known in the 19th Century mainly for his religious music which is rich and very beautiful. This exceptionally demanding little secular song uses an almost incomprehensible text by the poet Shelley.

Adiemus ... ... *Karl Jenkins*
A great favourite with the choir, Adiemus became well-known from its use in TV commercials. The words recall the sound of Latin and of the South Seas but are actually quite meaningless. Nevertheless one senses in the music an underlying message of peace and fraternity. We sing three of its many movements ....
Adiemus - Amaté adea - Cantus iteratus

O Nata Lux ... ... *Thomas Tallis*
Foremost English composer of the 17th Century, Thomas Tallis typified the age of polyphony with a style that is frequently complex and hard to perform. O Nata Lux is a short motet which we sing, not in its original five parts, but re-arranged into two semi-choruses of three parts each.

Staging arrangements

When deciding on your seating/standing arrangements for rehearsals, keep in mind the relative strength and weakness of individual singers. If a particular section has only a few reliable singers, place them in the middle of the section. If there are equal numbers of strong and weak, mix them up well - don't let all the older ones gather in the back row. Do tell them why, though; they'd rather sit with their friends but will understand the need for their leadership to be distributed through the choir. If the whole section is strong with just a few passengers, put the weak ones in the centre of the section. Obvious, really. Apart from that, it is normal to have younger ones in front because they are shorter and have a higher AQ ("aaaah!" quotient). Why miss the simplest trick in appealing to your audience?

In rehearsal it works well to have only two or at most three long rows of chairs, curved sharply so that they virtually surround you when you conduct. It helps their ensemble if they can see each other across the room. None of them are far away from you, which means that you can hear individuals quite easily and it also cuts down on inattentiveness and little conversations in the back row. Do, however, try to space the chairs out as much as you can within the confines of the room. You don't want them to become too dependent on their neighbours, and they need to be able to hear themselves as well as others.

In performance, however, narrow and deep is preferable. If suitable staging is available, four or even five shortish rows is good for ensemble in a large, resonant space. Good staging is very important, of course. Height is not an issue (steps as small as six inches are fine) but depth is, because each row needs enough space in front of it to wield the music. Safety is important, too. Are they likely to fall off the back and injure themselves? Is the stage going to collapse, in which case you may find yourself getting publicity of the wrong sort in the local newspaper? Nearly as bad, are there loose planks that are going to make a dreadful noise every time somebody steps on them? One has, of course, to be flexible. Sometimes staging is not available at all, in which case one must do the best one can. If you are performing in a church there may be useful steps at the entrance to the chancel (the bit where the choir-stalls usually are) or, further back, a single step at the entrance to the sanctuary. Otherwise you need to consider doing without different levels altogether.

Performing "on the flat" is not only perfectly possible, some choir trainers and their choirs prefer it. Revert to your rehearsal pattern of two or three long rows, curved at the ends towards the conductor, and make them spread out as much as they possibly can so that the rear rows can look at you between the front row. I have seen choirs perform very well indeed while standing as much as six feet away from each other, and experienced singers might enjoy this as they will be able to hear themselves really well - try it in rehearsal. With a little jiggling about they will all be able to see and be seen. It can certainly save a lot of fuss, as you can walk into any building and perform at the drop of a hat.

Once your repertoire for the term is fairly well established and preferably memorised, try singing "scrambled". This means arranging the choir (or allowing it to arrange itself) so that no singer is standing next to another on the same part. This frightens them at first - it frightens adult amateurs even more - but once they find they can do it, they love it. The singers in my older choir constantly beg to sing scrambled, and in one of the junior choirs I used to have one little girl who was often to be found sitting in the wrong place. When you said "Helen, you're a second soprano. Why are you sitting with the altos?" she'd reply "I'm singing scrambled!" She was, too.

In performance, scrambled singing is the ultimate. It means that every singer is able to be self-reliant, that every singer can hear the other parts around them which can and does improve overall intonation, and that the resulting sound is rich and well-blended although I have heard it said that audiences find it confusing because they can't tell who they're supposed to be listening to! But watch out - sometimes individual singers feel the need to work too hard which makes them unduly prominent.

In buildings that lend themselves to it, don't forget the possibility of antiphonal singing - half the choir in one place, half the choir in another, perhaps at the front and back of a church. This is a spectacular way to start a concert - the audience think "Oh, this is a very small choir?" and then realise that there are more angelic voices coming from behind them! Some buildings will not allow this to work successfully, however, and trial and error is needed to see whether the singers can hear each other or see you sufficiently well to make it hang together.

Judging the acoustics of a new building is quite difficult. For all the research that has presumably been done it remains an imperfect science, and few of us can walk into a strange place and say with any certainty "Yes, this'll sound wonderful". They say Benjamin Britten could do it, but I certainly can't. Buildings vary for all sorts of incomprehensible reasons. The best acoustic I ever encountered was at Lismore Cathedral in Eire, where the sound of the choir was so ravishing I had to stop the rehearsal and go outside for a minute to recover my composure. The worst was in another very big church, the Cathedral of S.Ouen in Rouen in Normandy, where you felt that every sound you made was being sucked right out of your mouth and vanishing into the air – quite horrid.

One architectural feature that often makes difficulties is the proscenium arch. In a theatre this is the front opening between the hall and the stage. If you stand your choir behind it, some of their sound may be trapped behind the arch and not reach the audience at all, especially if there are stage curtains and draperies around. The answer here is to move the choir as far forward as you can, so they are either right under the archway or out in front of it if the stage has a front apron. A similar feature can be found in many churches, and this is the archway at the entrance to the chancel, where, in most English churches anyway, the building becomes much narrower. This can also trap some sound, and you should experiment to see if you need to move the choir nearer the audience. Cruciform churches (those built in the shape of a cross) often have a high vault or dome over the crossing, and strangely there can sometimes be an acoustical "dead spot" directly underneath this. If in doubt, move the choir around during rehearsal and listen to the effect, or get someone else to.

It's always worthwhile setting the choir singing and then walking away down the hall for a good listen. Ideally you want a little "looseness" - just the suspicion of an echo which will enhance the sound and iron out any little defects. The kind of acoustic that suits speech or an orchestra is often a little "dry" for us. When listening to your choir in a new building, pay most attention to the clarity of the words. If the words are less clear than usual, the acoustic is probably "taking the top off" - in other words, it is not transmitting/reflecting the higher frequencies. In this case, make the choir work hard on their diction, bringing the sound out in front of their faces and smiling a lot to brighten the sound. And for your own part, reduce the tempo slightly in your fast pieces.

On the other hand if the words are nice and clear the acoustic must be good, so maintain your tempi and concentrate on smooth, beautiful sound rather than detail. Do talk to your choir about acoustics, and explain to them the likely effects - "can you hear yourself more than usual? Can you hear the altos? Can you hear the piano? Is it a nice place to sing in? This is what we're going to have to do about it ....."

Movements and choreography

Audiences love to see movement during a performance, and children enjoy it too, although adolescents can be embarrassed. Movement can range from small head or hand movements, through appropriate adjustments to posture at particular places, all the way to elaborate choreographed routines such as the marvellous performances one sometimes sees from adult "barbershop" choirs like "Shannon Express". Songs that include clapping or finger-snapping are a good way to start.

Whether you decide to go down this route depends on your own skills and experience. If, like me, you find it hard to think of appropriate movements, I suggest you should forget it and concentrate on the music instead - there is nothing sadder than to see a choir doing mechanical movements that have little or nothing to do with the song, just because their conductor thinks they ought to be doing something. Any movements must arise from the music, and must not interfere with it so contorted postures and movements that turn the face away from the audience are out of the question.

But even if you have decided to eschew choreographed movement, this does not mean that your choir need be completely static. As we said earlier in the section about "communication", natural movements of face and head must always be a good thing if they serve to help the singers "feel" the music for themselves and communicate it to the audience. A totally wooden choir is very boring, and the audience need something to look at while they listen!

Singing with an orchestra

DON'T DO IT! Or at least make sure it's a small ensemble, and choose your music carefully. While some composers certainly have the knack of writing for choir and orchestra so that the two are not in direct competition - Britten springs to mind, and Orff's *Carmina Burana* usually works well in this respect - others don't. The exciting *Dies Irae* from Verdi's *Requiem*, wonderful though it is, is one famous place where there is absolutely no way the choir can make enough noise to cope. I suspect that most professional recordings of this work are enhanced in the studio, because I have never been able to hear the choir all through in a live performance.

You just can't win. Any decent sized orchestra can always make enough noise to drown even the strongest choir. Youth orchestras especially find it hard to even approach a decent *piano* when playing *tutti*. If you had a youth orchestra of, say, 70 players and a choir twice that size you might manage a decent balance, but otherwise ...... no chance! The laws of physics apply here. It is easy enough to imagine that if you have one flautist playing in a room, and then add a second flautist, the total volume of sound will not double. It will actually only increase by about ten percent. Two more flautists will add another ten percent, and so on in a kind of geometrical progression. In practice, to double the amount of sound a choir can make you would probably need four or five times the number of singers, and who can find that many?

Many orchestral conductors are inept at dealing with young singers, and will often make unreasonable demands on them. Youth orchestra section coaches are even worse! Don't allow these people to interfere with your choir by telling them they can't be heard (that's the orchestra's fault). Or that they aren't smiling (they aren't supposed to, at least not if the music/words don't demand it). Or that they aren't watching (they should be, but it's your job to correct this). Or that the words can't be heard (ditto). When I find myself in this position - one I always try to avoid - I give my choir a standing instruction beforehand that if anyone asks them to sing louder, they are not to do so. They must concentrate even more on the clarity of their diction, they must get their heads up and out of their copies, they must think hard about all the things they have rehearsed, but they must NOT on any account try to sing louder.

If you absolutely have to make your choir sing behind a large orchestra in the normal configuration, keep your singers away from the French Horns. Their bells point backwards, and a strong horn section at full blast (and they usually <u>are</u> at full blast) can project an amount of sound straight at your front-row sopranos that is positively painful. I have known singers faint or leave the stage in tears, and it wasn't until I actually went to sit beside them that I realised why.

And beware - the first time your choir encounter the orchestra will probably be disastrous. They will feel nervous, they will be distracted by all that is going on around them, they will be put off by orchestra members turning round and staring - how do orchestral players of all ages manage to look so disapproving and bored all the time? I know they aren't really, because I used to be one! Orchestras frequently rehearse in rooms that are not acoustically ideal for a choir, which doesn't help. You will feel that they are being viewed critically, and you will be on tenterhooks ready to leap in and defend them from any abuse. The whole experience is likely to be quite demoralising for them and you.

There are two thing you can do to counter this. One is to discuss it with the choir first; tell them what's going to happen, describe what they are going to see and warn them how it will feel. The other is to build them up beforehand;

make sure they know their parts inside out and backwards, try to see that they can sing from memory if possible, and boost their morale - they have been specially chosen to do this, they are the bee's knees, they're doing the orchestra/choral society a great favour by condescending to help out with this little show, the orchestra may not be good enough to accompany us properly so we'll have to magnanimously sing even better to make up for their shortcomings - in other words, lie shamelessly and without compunction. Assuming it <u>is</u> a lie, of course ....

When things go wrong

It is vital that we and our choirs recognise that absolute perfection is beyond our reach most of the time, although that shouldn't stop us trying. Things will go wrong, despite your best efforts and those of your singers. "S**t happens!" is a favourite expression among some of my pupils.

There are two main things that go wrong in concerts.

The first is that children feel unwell or faint. The lights are hot, it's been a long day, they haven't been feeling well anyway, they are starting their period, they are nervous or excited, they've been on their feet for the last twenty-five minutes .... There was a time years ago that we hardly ever had a major concert without at least one child fainting. We used to post a member of staff on each side of the choir to catch them and help them off!

Nowadays my choirs have a standing (ha! ha!) instruction that if, during a concert, they feel the need to sit down for a bit, they must do so immediately - on their chair, on the step of the staging, or just on the floor, wherever it will cause the least fuss. There are no heroics, no "the show must go on!", and no sense of failure or criticism - this is a perfectly normal thing to do in a concert, so far as we are concerned. The concert continues uninterrupted, and when they feel better they just stand again and join in. The alternative is that sickly children will either faint or have to leave the stage with the risk that your performance is disrupted and concentration broken. You will have to put a member of staff or parent in the changing room to look after them. The singers and their parents may begin to question whether this choir thing is such a good idea after all if it has such a terrible effect on them. So ..... don't risk it. Rely on them to be sensible, and they will be.

The other thing that can go wrong is musical breakdown. This is also inevitable at some time or other. One section may miss an entry, or you may forget to bring them in and they won't have the nerve to do it by themselves (they should, of course: have you been nurse-maiding them too much?) One of the inside parts may just lose its way and stop singing. Your accompanist may forget a repeat and cause confusion. <u>You</u> may forget a repeat and cause

115

confusion! In an unaccompanied piece the choir may go disastrously flat. Often you can survive this and many people in the audience may not even notice, but if the choir gradually get so flat that they no longer find the notes in the part of their voices they normally expect, it can cause breakdown.

The main thing here is damage limitation. You must do whatever will cause the least disruption to the performance as a whole, and whatever will cause the least loss of confidence in your choir. Above all, do not display annoyance or criticism. And try not to allow your choir time to become upset about it - move quickly and get on with the performance.

If the error is a small one and hasn't stopped the other sections, you may be able to keep going and ride over it in the hope that the offending section will pick themselves up and get back in. If you are wise you will have practised this sort of recovery in rehearsal by *not stopping for every mistake*. Make the point to your singers that even the best musicians make mistakes, and that they are allowed to make mistakes as well. But it is the mark of the really good musician that he or she is flexible and intelligent enough to recover from errors quickly and calmly - and that's just what they'll do. If you think it's necessary, don't be afraid to step a little nearer to the section in trouble and help them by singing their part for a bar or two until they recover. The audience may not notice.

If you judge that it is necessary to stop, do so. Say nothing, just use your hands to signal a pause. Smile, however furious you are inside. Pick a suitable place you know they can all find easily, and tell them in a clear voice "Starting again from letter C, middle of page 13!" and begin again. Try to let as little time elapse as possible, so that there is less of a hiatus, and the choir will be too busy singing to worry about what went wrong. You can help make this damage-limitation process more effective by moving quickly during rehearsal. Don't hang around repeating the bar number or page number umpteen times because the back row of the altos are busy having a little conversation, just say it once and start - and when the altos suddenly come to and don't know where they are, give them a hard time about it! They will soon become aware that you expect concentration all through the rehearsal, not just during the singing. This alertness will stand you in good stead if you have trouble during a concert.

I only once remember having to completely abandon a piece during a concert. It was a difficult piece which neither I nor the children liked very much (so why the hell were we doing it, I wonder?) and after it had broken down twice it was obvious that there was no point in going on as the choir were getting rattled. I hope I dealt with it calmly and with a minimum of fuss. I think I turned to the audience and took the blame myself with some lame crack like "Terribly sorry, ladies and gentlemen, the conductor's brain stopped! We'll go on to the next piece ...." The audience probably guessed that it wasn't really my fault, and the choir guessed that the audience had guessed that it wasn't my fault, but everyone's face was saved a little (including mine, as nobody believed it was my fault at all and they thought I was being magnanimous in taking the blame). Oh, what games we play ....!

Nerves

I suppose it's all right for <u>you</u> to feel nervous before a performance. Personally I find competitions harder than concerts - one knows that one's work is being critically heard not only by the adjudicators but by other choir-trainers who would probably be quite pleased if you went wrong! There is one simple trick that will help your choir not to feel nervous when they stand up before an audience: "attack is the best form of defence".

It is entirely natural for children to be embarrassed on such occasions, and one should discuss this with them quite seriously. But it's hard to feel embarrassed if you yourself are deliberately embarrassing someone else. Demonstrate this to them - fix one of them with your eye, sing right at them, mouthing the words very clearly and not taking your gaze away for a moment. He or she will probably go red and giggle! It can be very embarrassing and even a little scary to have someone singing right at you and focusing all their attention on you.

So your choir's task is simple. Each of them has to pick a person in the audience - someone they don't know, and not too near the front (we're not <u>really</u> trying to intimidate the audience, more to sort of "un-intimidate" the choir) - and sing every word and every note right between their eyes. Provided every choir-member does this right at the beginning of the concert, they'll look confident, sound confident and feel confident. You can help the choir by choosing an opening number which starts with a strong *tutti* entry.

It's also worth pointing out to the choir that they do really want the audience to <u>like</u> them. So once the beginning of the concert has passed, once your singers have got into their stride and have the audience right where they want them, they can start to think about charming them a bit. Ask them to think about their own friends - if there were someone in their class who never smiled at them and never looked them in the eye, what are the chances of any friendship developing? Very small, I should think. Therefore they need (a) to make eye contact with their audience - suggest that each of them picks say, three audience members (again, not too near the front) and looks at each one from time to time - and (b) to smile at the audience <u>sometimes</u>. Of course <u>we</u> know that they'll be smiling because the vowel sounds demand it, or when they need to maintain the pitch, but the audience won't know that.

My junior choirs practise this routinely right from the start. We make one of the children sit out in front and sing to her; sometimes we enlist the aid of a parent and try to (a) embarrass and then (b) charm them. I've even used a large teddy bear which we named and gave a woolly hat in the choir's signature colour (pink, what else?).

Summary

- *Don't sing out of doors*

- *Publicity rarely works, but do it anyway*

- *Whatever you feel about choral competitions in principle, in practice they are really good fun and can breed confidence*

- *How your choir get on and off the stage is not as important as the quality of their singing, but it comes pretty close*

- *Be very cautious about fitting in with other people's performance plans. Your choir is the most important thing*

- *Foreign tours are hard work but very worthwhile. Don't try to do it alone, though*

- *Put a lot of thought into your concert-planning. The shorter the programme the more your audience will love you!*

- *Staging - do you really need it?*

- *Never perform in a building you haven't inspected first*

- *Singing with an orchestra - DON'T!*

- *Plan in advance what you will do if something goes wrong. Sooner or later, it will*

- *Encourage your singers to think about, plan and practise their relationship with the audience*

CODA - CARING FOR YOUR CHOIR

Things to tell a choir off for:

- Inattention

- Fidgeting

- Chattering

- Forgetting what they practised last week

- Singing too loudly

Things <u>not</u> to tell a choir off for

- Singing out of tune (but it's OK to criticise the reason - such as forgetting to breathe properly)

- Singing wrong notes

- Not singing loud enough. <u>NEVER tell a choir off for not singing loud enough</u>. That comes from practice, good technique, knowing the music really well and liking it, and confidence in themselves engendered by much praise and good experiences of performance. It does not come from effort, and if they have to make much of an effort, intonation and tone will suffer. <u>Power comes from the warm-up.</u>

Things not to let <u>other people</u> tell your choir off for

- Not singing loud enough

- Not smiling

- Not singing loud enough

- Not singing loud enough

Love your choir

It's a strange thing to want to do, singing.

Choral singers are frequently undervalued especially by instrumentalists (and many music teachers). They think that because everyone has a voice, singing must be an easy option.

Singers are abused by almost everyone. The orchestral conductor who shouts and raves when your choir of thirty dewy-eyed 12-year-old girls can't make themselves heard on a bottom D over his 90-strong symphony orchestra all playing a solid *forte* (the only dynamic they know). The headmaster who gives them a pep-talk before the concert that ends with "come on, sing up AND FOR GOD'S SAKE SMILE, THIS ISN'T A FUNERAL!". The elderly lady who complains that she couldn't hear every single word and why didn't that girl at the front have her shirt tucked in? Other children who think singing is soppy. Other children who play instruments and still think singing is soppy. I have even had parents - normally your greatest supporters - put considerable pressure on their daughter to leave the choir in case it interfered with her violin playing.

Don't these people know how hard singing is? That it is physically tiring, emotionally draining and hurts your feet? That it requires a peculiar kind of manic self-confidence to stand up and make a fool of yourself in public using your own voice? That it requires teamwork par excellence, the selfless desire to subvert your own will to that of the group for the good of the group? That it represents the best possible aural, oral, personal, social and musical training you can have?

I really can't understand why children want to do it. I am just glad they do. And they deserve all the support, praise, encouragement and love you can give them just for being there in your rehearsals week after week.

So do it - build them up, tell them how fantastic they are, tell them their parents will love it, tell them you can't believe they have been so clever as to learn this song all through in only seventeen and a half months, tell them that no-one can possibly notice that the altos are a minor third flat most of the time and anyway a minor third is quite normal for an alto, tell them you've got the entire 2009 Choir of the Year on video and the winners weren't a patch on them, promise them fame, sweets, money, anything to keep them happy, keep them working, keep them interested, keep them achieving, keep them there. They're wonderful. But you know that bit on page three where the second sopranos come in? Well, it could just be a teeny bit more secure so we'd just better do it one more time ....

Children do best, the things they are best at. They do them and keep on doing them, not just to earn praise or pocket money, but because they love to do something really well. The boy who spends hours alone in the back garden, keeping his football constantly in the air with foot and head and knee, does so because it is wonderful and absorbing and fun just to be able to do it. The child who drives you mad playing "Chopsticks" over and over again on the piano is not doing it because he thinks it's a great tune (it isn't), and not because his friends like it (they don't), and not because it annoys you (it does) but because he can.

Your task as a choir-trainer is to foster in your pupils their own enjoyment of, and fascination with, the things they can do. To do this you need to put them in touch with their own ability, make them hear themselves as you hear them, and allow them to realise that what they have already learned to do is something very special, quite out of the ordinary and way beyond the normal attainment of their peers. You do it by the obvious means of praising and encouraging them, as well as by ensuring that you place them in situations where others - parents, audiences, the local press, competition judges and so on - will praise them and make a fuss of them too.

But more than this, you must employ techniques in your rehearsals that enable them to listen to themselves. For instance, instead of having them face you all the time, make them stand in a circle and sing to each other without this large hairy extrovert prancing about in front and distracting them. If you can do so without causing too much disruption, encourage individual children to leave their places and stand beside you listening, so they can hear the whole effect as you do. In my junior girls' choirs which each have a single rather long practice each week, it has become normal for girls to leave the room to visit the lavatory or refill their water-bottles without asking (they've always been very sensible and the building is secure, so why should I make an issue of it?). Every ten or fifteen minutes one of them will quietly leave her place and go out, and often on her return will stand inside the door, or look over my shoulder as I play the piano, or just plop herself down in a chair in the corner and listen to the rehearsal for a few minutes before resuming her own place. In this way they learn to appreciate the overall effect, and know what contribution is made by each individual to the whole - and, I hope, they hear and enjoy how very good their singing is.

This is not to say that they should not be encouraged to be self-critical, or that you should never criticise them. The boy who keeps the football in the air is doubtless very critical of himself when he drops it. By all means criticise your singers in round and colourful terms when they "drop it" and demand that they do better, but try to make sure that they know what they did wrong and what they have to do to make it better. I once sat in on a rehearsal where the choir sang all the way through *Beatus Vir*. When they got to the end, the conductor said "Well, that wasn't very good. Do it again, and do it better!". They did, and it wasn't, because he hadn't told them how.

When children are listening to themselves they need to know what to listen for - are they in tune with each other? are they in tune with the piano? is their ensemble really tight? are the words sufficiently clear? are there any breaths in the obvious wrong places? do their faces have the right expression for the pitch and the diction? etc. etc. But our young footballer also thinks to himself "Cor, two hundred and seventy-eight bounces without once touching the floor! I am just so <u>good</u> at this!" Hand-in-hand with the critical faculty goes the ability to know when you are doing something really well, and to get a kick out of it.

That's all I have to say. Enjoy.

A little round for your choir to sing. If you can't photocopy it, send a large stamped, addressed envelope to Choirmaster Press, Harmony House, 10 Walnut Tree Meadow, Stonham Aspal, Stowmarket, Suffolk IP14 6DF, UK and we'll post you a copy ....

A Silly Little Ditty

for Ipswich Girls' Choir, who deserve it

David Bramhall

Appendix One: Tonic Sol-fa or *solfège*

This old method of describing the steps of the scale used to be very common. In my youth I remember singing in choirs beside elderly choristers who did not read conventional notation at all, but had special editions of the music written entirely in solfa. The complexity of, say, Handel's "Messiah" written entirely in solfa seemed very daunting to me at the time, and seems unnecessary to me now.

However, very often solfa names are still the most convenient way of describing notes and I have used them in this book in a few places. Therefore if you're not familiar with the system you need to know that each step of the scale has its own solfa name, as follows .....

The names remain the same even if the scale is different – for instance, in the key of D the key note is still called "doh" and the third is still "me" ....

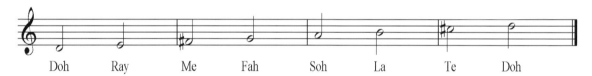

This is known as the "moveable doh" system, espoused by the great John Curwen in his famous choral method. There is, or was, a "fixed doh" system as well. Doesn't bear thinking about, really.

That's all you need to know, except that in the minor scale the crucial minor third is called "mor" ....

.... which is very appropriate – "me" sounds bright and sharp which is just what a major third should be, while the darker sound of the minor third is aptly described by the sombre word "mor".

Appendix Two: Some other books to read ...

This is not a proper bibliography, just some random comments on books I have bought and found useful (or not) ...

"Choral Music Experience ... education through artistry" Volume 5 "The Young Singing Voice" by Doreen Rao, published by Boosey & Hawkes.
You have to admire the American way of stringing large numbers of words together without making any discernible sense. The very title of this slim book is magnificently meaningless. Why not ...

"Choral Music Education ... artistry through experience"? Or ...

"Choral Artistry ... education through musical experience"? Or ...

"Artistry ... choral experience through music education"? Or ....

Doreen Rao is on much firmer ground once she stops trying to justify herself – as if, with her worldwide reputation, she needed to – and gets to some photos of real children standing nicely and doing real singing, and quotes the musical exercises they are doing. The sections on "Exercise", "Posture" and "Breathing" are good, but the section on "Tone" suffers from a tendency to state what ought to be obvious – *"the student's ability to manipulate the vowel results in a specific tonal effect"*. Yeah, right. The exercises under "Vocalisation" are sound but few in number.

On the whole, not an essential purchase and in parts very annoying. I don't like paying good money to be advised to ask myself *"where does the material lie? Is it high? Is it low?"* I think I'd worked that out for myself.

"Giving Voice – a handbook for choir directors and trainers" by David Hill, Hilary Parfitt and Elizabeth Ash, published by Kevin Mayhew.
This book is mainly directed at trainers of church choirs. It is beautifully and clearly written, and intelligently illustrated with appropriate sketches and musical examples. There are many useful musical exercises. A pleasure to read and own, and recommended for all choir-trainers.

"Lifeline for Children's Choir Directors" by Jean Ashworth Bartle, published by Gordon V.Thompson Music (I bought mine from William Elkin, 31 Exchange Street, Norwich NR2 1DP Tel.01603 666332).

Jean Ashworth Bartle is the doyenne of Canadian choir-trainers and directs the famous Toronto Children's Chorus. This rather expensive book is a mixed blessing. On the one hand it is massive and thorough, while on the other it shares Doreen Rao's penchant for the unnecessary or the embarrassingly trite (*"... volunteers are like Coke – they're the real thing"*).

There is much advice on peripheral matters like numbering every choir seat and keeping a register, and not many solid suggestions about actual singing, although the few that do occur are excellent – her explanation of diphthongs is the clearest I have seen. There are colossal though rather out-dated lists of repertoire and a couple of excellent bibliographies, but on the whole I have difficulty with a book that spends 34 lines on making choir "vests" and only 14 on the reasons for flat singing!

"Kick-start your Choir – confidence-boosting strategies" by Mike Brewer, published by Faber.
Nobody knows his subject better than Michael Brewer, Director of the National Youth Choir of Great Britain, and this slim volume is direct, chatty and packed with really sensible advice. Every choir-trainer should buy a copy (maybe they already have?) and it's cheap, too. I just wish it was longer - a serious, detailed discussion of the subject by this author would be well worth reading.

"John Bertalot's Immediately Practical Tips for Choral Directors" and "How to be a Successful Choir Director" by John Bertalot, published by Augsburg Fortress

I must be honest and admit that I have not read either of these books. However, John Bertalot is well-known in the field and certainly knows what he's talking about.

Here is one reader's review of "How to be a successful choir director", taken from the Amazon website ...

John Bertalot's previous book "Immediately practical tips for choral conductors" contained a lot of information about all aspects of running a choir, from warm-ups and rehearsals to support groups and more general public relations. The problem was that it was written in a chatty narrative style that made it almost unreadable, and the absence of informative chapter titles or an index meant that it was impossible to find information when you went back to the book.

All these faults have been corrected in "How to Be a Successful Choir Director", the book is a mine of no-nonsense information that can be put into practice at your next rehearsal. All aspects of choral conducting and choir training are explained with great clarity, and the well thought out chapter headings mean that when you have a particular problem, you know where to look for the solution.

In short, an indispensable book for any aspiring choir director, and one that many choirs might consider buying for their director.

Printed in Great Britain
by Amazon.co.uk, Ltd.,
Marston Gate.